MW00719307

THE SOVIET IMPACT
ON THE
WESTERN WORLD

BY

EDWARD HALLETT CARR
Professor of International Politics
in the University College of Wales

NEW YORK

THE MACMILLAN COMPANY

1947

Copyright, 1947, by
THE MACMILLAN COMPANY.

All rights reserved—no part of this book
may be reproduced in any form without
permission in writing from the publisher,
except by a reviewer who wishes to quote brief
passages in connection with a review written
for inclusion in magazine or newspaper.

First Printing.

PRINTED IN THE UNITED STATES OF AMERICA

The six chapters of this small volume have their origin in six lectures delivered in Oxford in February and March, 1946, for the Estlin Carpenter Trust and printed here without substantial change. A considerable part of Chapter I was also included in the Cust Foundation Lecture delivered in November, 1945, at University College, Nottingham, on "Democracy in International Affairs" and published in pamphlet form by the College. The author is indebted to the College for courteous permission to reprint this material in the present volume.

INTRODUCTION

THE impact of the Soviet Union on the western world has been a decisive historical event, though it may be difficult to assess its consequences with precision. Even in the physical sciences, where experiments can be repeated and results verified, the relation of cause and effect seems today more tenuous and more uncertain than it seemed to our forefathers. In history the relation is more problematical still: indeed it can very well be argued that cause and effect in history are only the more or less arbitrary pattern into which the historian weaves events in order to render them significant. Unless, however, we are content to believe that history has no meaning, we are bound to treat it as a coherent sequence in which one set of events or ideas leads on to another set of events or ideas and helps to influence and determine them; and among the influences which have helped to mould the western world in the last quarter of a century the Bolshevik Revolution and its aftermath occupy an outstanding place.

A certain vagueness must be allowed for, even in the definition of the subject. Sometimes Soviet influence has been transmitted to western Europe through other countries, notably Germany; conversely, the Soviet impact has sometimes been the impact of ideas which once had their origin in western Europe but, having been forgotten or neglected there, were applied, transformed and re-exported to the west by the Bolshevik Revolution. Moreover, even if it can be demonstrated that certain developments in the Soviet Union point the

vii

way to analogous developments a few years later in the western world, it will no doubt be open to the critic to say that these western events or tendencies were not the effect of Soviet example, but that some remoter cause was producing similar effects successively in different countries. But even where this is true—and in some cases it probably is true—Soviet experience will still be significant and suggestive for much that is happening or seems likely to happen in the west. The chapters which follow, while they can do no more than skim the surface of a vast subject, are an attempt to investigate, not the merits or demerits of the Soviet achievement, but the extent of its significance for western civilization.

CONTENTS

PAGE

I. THE POLITICAL IMPACT   1

II. THE ECONOMIC IMPACT   20

III. THE SOCIAL IMPACT   42

IV. THE IMPACT ON INTERNATIONAL RELATIONS   62

V. THE IDEOLOGICAL IMPACT   84

VI. SOME HISTORICAL PERSPECTIVES   103

THE SOVIET IMPACT
ON THE WESTERN WORLD

I

THE POLITICAL IMPACT

THE political impact of the Soviet Union on the western world came at a moment of crisis in the fortunes of democracy. Outwardly triumphant in 1918, the high tide of democracy ebbed with bewildering rapidity; and the period between the two wars was one of disappointment and discouragement for the supporters of democracy. Not only were democratic institutions abandoned in a large number of countries, great and small, but even in those countries which maintained them, faith in democracy often seemed to flag and to lose its former vitality and self-confidence. It became a commonplace to say that democracy had failed to solve social and economic problems and that political democracy was not enough; and a well-known British champion of democracy voiced a common feeling in the nineteen-thirties when he wrote that "we are uncertain what the democracy is for which we stand".[1] Today, when the open enemies of democracy have once more been overthrown in a victorious war, western democracy is confronted by a new challenge from a country which purports to be the pioneer of a new and more progressive form of democracy—Soviet democracy.

The actuality of the challenge can be pointed by a curious

[1] R. H. S. Crossman, *Plato To-Day*, p. 292. Other quotations of a similar tenor will be found in E. H. Carr, *Conditions of Peace*, p. 15.

comparison which has hitherto been little noticed. It was Woodrow Wilson who, in the middle of the first world war, threw the word "democracy" into the international arena by proclaiming it as an allied war aim, coined the famous phrase, "The world must be made safe for democracy", and declared that future peace could only be secured by "a partnership of democratic nations". His insistence on dealing at the time of the armistice only with a constitutionally elected German Government had beyond doubt a great deal to do with the establishment of the Weimar republic. The victory of November 1918 came to be commonly regarded as the victory of democracy; and the new states which arose all over central and eastern Europe hastened to equip themselves with democratic constitutions. The sequel provided little incentive between the two wars to invoke the slogan of democracy in international affairs, though it was used on occasion in the middle and later 30's to justify "popular front" movements— significantly enough, under Soviet inspiration. Nor did much come of an attempt in the early stages of the second world war to represent the allies as champions of democracy—if only because it was important to conciliate certain non-democratic countries. The Atlantic Charter, predominantly Wilsonian though it was in ideas and phraseology, made no mention of democracy.

It was Marshal Stalin who, consciously or unconsciously usurping Woodrow Wilson's role in the previous war, once more placed democracy in the forefront of allied war aims. In his broadcast of July 3, 1941, he spoke of the Soviet war against Hitler being "merged with the struggle of the peoples of Europe and America for independence and democratic liberty"; and on November 6, 1942, he described the restoration of "democratic liberties" in Europe as one of the aims of the Anglo-Soviet-American coalition. The first mention of democracy in an international instrument relating to war aims occurred in the Stalin-Sikorski declaration of December 4, 1941, which proclaimed that "a just and durable peace" can be guaranteed only "by a new organization of international relations based on an enduring alliance between the democratic countries"—an echo, almost a quotation, of Wilson's phrase of 1917. At successive conferences the three Great Powers commended democracy to the world. At Moscow in November 1943 they demanded that the Italian Government should be "made more democratic". At Teheran a month later they looked forward to "a world family of democratic nations". At Yalta they announced their intention of "meeting the political and economic problems of liberated Europe in accordance with democratic principles": they would assist the European nations "to solve by democratic means their present political and economic problems" and to "create democratic institutions of their own choice". More specifically the Polish Government was to be "reorganized on a broader democratic basis" and "all democratic and anti-nazi parties" were to have the right to participate in the elections. The Potsdam Declaration of August 1945 transferred the principle to Germany: German education was to be "so controlled as completely to eliminate nazi and militarist doctrines and to make possible the successful development of democratic ideas"; the judicial system was to be reorganized "in accordance with the principles of democracy"; local self-government was to be restored "on democratic principles"; and encouragement was to be given throughout Germany to "all democratic political parties". These texts, the Soviet inspiration of which was no secret, had one general significance. The missionary role which had been filled in the first world war by American democracy and Woodrow Wilson had passed in the second world war to Soviet democracy and Marshal Stalin. In 1919 democratic institutions on the model of western democracy were installed in many countries: in 1945 the new political institutions which arose in eastern Europe—not to speak of those which had arisen ten or more years earlier in parts of China—conformed, though rather less slavishly, to the Soviet pattern.

The challenge thus boldly thrown into the international arena was not in itself new. It had·been announced by no one more clearly than by Lenin himself. The two following quotations may be taken as typical:

"Proletarian democracy is a million times more democratic than any *bourgeois* democracy; the Soviet power is a million times more democratic than the most democratic *bourgeois* republic."

"The Soviet system is the maximum of democracy for the workers and peasants; at the same time it means a break with *bourgeois* democracy and the rise of a *new* universal-historical *type* of democracy, namely, proletarian democracy or the dictatorship of the proletariat."

It is in the same spirit that Stalin in his speech on the new constitution of 1936 described it as "the only thoroughly democratic constitution in the world". It would be a mistake to dismiss such pronouncements as mere propaganda or humbug. They show in the first place that Soviet leaders recognize degrees of democracy even in *bourgeois* society (both Marx and Lenin were always emphatic that *bourgeois* democracy represented an immense advance on feudalism) and, secondly, that they regard Soviet democracy as a new and more advanced species of democracy. It is therefore important to understand the nature, origins and distinguishing features of Soviet democracy.

It will probably be said at the outset that Soviet democracy inherits a Russian tradition. In Russia it has been customary throughout the ages to exalt the place of the community in social and political life and to stress the collective character

4

of rights and obligations; the strongly marked individualism implanted in the west by Renaissance and Reformation—the notion of the individual will as the supreme arbiter of human destiny and of the individual conscience as the ultimate moral censor—never penetrated the Russian tradition. On the other hand it will be said that the rulers of Russia have never been successful in working out a tolerable compromise between freedom and authority, freedom in Russia having always tended to degenerate into anarchy and authority into despotism, and that this failure is expressed in a general disrespect for law on the part of rulers who apply it capriciously and of subjects who readily evade it. These generalizations contain a particle of the truth. But it would be dangerous to treat Soviet democracy as primarily a Russian phenomenon without roots in the west or without application to western conditions. In fact, it is far less removed from one main stream of western democratic tradition than is often supposed.

.   .   .   .   .

Western democratic tradition admits two widely different conceptions of democracy deriving respectively from the English and French revolutions. In their origin the two revolutions exhibit a striking parallel. Both the English civil war and the French revolution were revolts by a nascent *bourgeoisie* against a legitimate monarchy based on an established church. The aim of both was to destroy the remnants of feudalism and establish the rule of the middle class. Cromwell was the true precursor of Robespierre, and both had marked traits which would in current terminology be called totalitarian. In both countries, revolutionary dictatorship was the instrument used to bring *bourgeois* democracy to birth—a striking historical precedent for the theories of Marx and Lenin.

Here, however, differences begin to emerge. Though the English civil war ended in the substantial victory of the new middle class, the victory was tempered by the survival of the monarchy in an attenuated but still powerful form. The issue had to be fought out again under James II, and the result was a compromise which left undisputed mastery to neither side. This was particularly true of the religious compromise between Anglicanism and dissent. The whole settlement, religious and political, strongly reflected the views of the dissenters who had preached toleration and the doctrine of the "inward light". The philosophy of English revolution as developed by Locke was based on the rights of the individual both against the church and against the state. Locke and his followers envisaged the state as a sort of wall or fence within which a society of individuals, guided by their own lights, conducted the essential processes of social life. The right to dissent—or in other words, the protection of minorities—is the essence of English democracy; and the rule of law means the enforcement of the rights of the individual against the state. Hence the feeling, rarely formulated quite explicitly but always latent in American if not in English politics, that democratic government means weak government, and that the less government there is, the more democracy there will be: hence also the pacifist streak that runs through English-speaking democracy.

Something of this spirit entered into the tradition of French democracy. Voltaire, who was temperamentally an extreme individualist, shared many of Locke's views on political liberty and on the right to dissent; and Voltaire's influence on French democracy remained powerful throughout the 19th century, finding its last conspicuous manifestation in the Dreyfus case. But Voltaire was the most intolerant of all advocates of toleration; and it was characteristic that the enemy of clericalism in France was not religious dissent—a possibility which had been destroyed by the expulsion of the Huguenots—but an

6

essentially dogmatic atheism. The predominant strain in French democracy as it emerged from the revolution was that not of Voltaire, but of Rousseau. Rousseau, in accepting the social contract, treated it, like Hobbes, as a final surrender by the individual of his rights against society. Rousseau, far from making the state a ring-fence to protect the working of a society of individuals, identified society with the state and posited an all-powerful "general will" from which it was treason to dissent. The spiritual father of the French revolution, he was also the father of modern totalitarian democracy.

The history of the revolution in France promoted the trend towards totalitarian democracy. The revolution began with the complete, sudden and irrevocable overthrow of the legitimate monarchy. As in England there was a royal execution; but in France the royal restoration of 1814 was no part of a national compromise, but a hollow sham forced on the country by foreign arms after the real issue of the revolution had been decided. Hence the French revolution, unlike the English, did not issue in a balance or compromise: it was a victory not for political toleration, or the rights of the individual as against the state, but for a particular view of the authority of the state.

All that the revolution did [a recent historian of French political thought has remarked] was to transfer the existing system from one nominal ruler to another, to substitute "popular" for "royal" sovereignty, to give to the "people" the powers hitherto enjoyed by the crown—but without any challenging or questioning of those powers in themselves.[1]

The association of revolutionary democracy with absolute power was the lesson of Napoleon's astonishing career. In Guizot's trenchant words:

[1] R. Soltau: *French Political Thought in the Nineteenth Century*, p. xx.

7

Absolute power cannot belong in France except to the Revolution and its heirs, for they alone, for many years to come, can re-assure the masses about their interests while refusing them guarantees of liberty.[1]

It was in keeping with this tradition that France produced in the person of Napoleon III the first modern "democratic" dictator.

What I have called the English conception of democracy had little influence in Europe in the half century after the French revolution; for few people would at this time have called Great Britain a democracy.[2] Throughout this period the word democracy was used throughout Europe by friend or foe alike in the sense consecrated by the revolution, and retained its revolutionary connotation unchallenged till after 1848. "Gegen Demokraten helfen nur Soldaten" was an aphorism attributed to Friedrich Wilhelm I of Prussia. Marx and Engels in the 'forties called themselves "democratic communists", and in the Communist Manifesto the phrases "to establish democracy" and "to raise the proletariat to the position of the ruling class" are equivalents. Before 1848 nobody had doubted that political democracy (one man, one vote) carried with it social democracy (equality or the levelling of classes), and that the progressive middle class which wanted universal suffrage was therefore fighting the cause of the masses. "Everyone without exception has the vote", declared the proclamation of the French Provisional Government of 1848. "Since this law has been announced, there are no longer any proletarians in France." [3] But this jubilation was prema-

---

[1] Guizot: *Mémoires pour servir à l'histoire de mon temps*, I, p. 34.
[2] Tocqueville, writing in the 1830's, called Great Britain with his customary insight "an aristocratic republic" (*De la Démocratie en Amérique*. (Paris 1835), II, p. 186).
[3] Lamartine, *Histoire de la Révolution de 1848*, p. 396.

ture. The middle class, having attained its primary objective and being frightened of the ulterior revolutionary aspirations of the masses, ceased to be revolutionary. In France it was quiescent, if not actively approving, when Cavaignac crushed the workers: and similar events happened all over Europe.

From 1848 onwards therefore political democracy ("liberal democracy") and social democracy ("socialism" or "communism") were to be found throughout Europe on opposite sides of the barricades. It was not that after 1848 "socialism" or "communism" became revolutionary (they always had been), but that "democracy" ceased to be revolutionary and tended more and more to be associated with conservatism. The name "social democrats" was adopted by the German workers' party in 1864, but accepted only under protest by Marx and Engels. The rift between "democracy" and "communism" *alias* "social democracy" was well under way. Napoleon III and Bismarck both showed that universal suffrage could be a powerful weapon against social democracy. In England, where there had been no 1848, the same developments followed later. The word democracy long remained in bad odour with the English ruling classes. Lord Salisbury could describe it contemptuously as a system under which "the rich would pay all the taxes and the poor make all the laws".[1] But by the turn of the century these inhibitions had been overcome; and since that time democracy has been continually invoked by conservatives, in England as elsewhere, as a bulwark of defence against the revolutionary onslaughts of socialism and communism.

Put therefore in its historical setting, the position of Soviet democracy is easy to understand. Always remote from the English revolutionary tradition, it belongs to the French revolutionary tradition of democracy as it existed in western

[1] Gwendolen Cecil, *Life of Robert Marquis of Salisbury*, I, p. 149.

Europe down to 1848. After 1848, according to the Soviet view, the *bourgeoisie* falsified and betrayed the democratic tradition by turning against the proletariat, and the victory of *bourgeois* democracy has not yet been completed and carried to its logical conclusion in western Europe by the victory of proletarian democracy or socialism. This conclusion has been reached only in Russia where the *bourgeois* revolution of March 1917 was quickly completed by the proletarian revolution of November 1917. The challenge which Soviet democracy presents to the western world is a challenge to complete the unfinished revolution.

The challenge may be considered under four heads; and under each of them some impact has already been made by the Soviet conception of democracy on the democracies of the west. The charges against western democracy are (1) that it remains purely formal and institutional and that the class content of the state is ignored, (2) that it remains purely political and does not extend to the social and economic plane, (3) that it lacks positive belief in itself, and is therefore dangerously tolerant of opposition, and (4) that it makes no provision for the participation of the masses in administration.

(1) Confusion of thought is often caused by the habit common among politicians and writers of the English-speaking world of defining democracy in formal and conventional terms as "self-government" or "government by consent". What these terms define is not democracy, but anarchy. Government of some kind is necessary in the common interest precisely because men will not govern themselves. "Government by consent" is a contradiction in terms; for the purpose of government is to compel people to do what they would not do of their own volition. In short, government is a process by which some people exercise compulsion on others. This is as true of democracy as of other forms of government; the

10

criteria are by whom, by what means, and for what, the compulsion is exercised. What determines the character of any government is, therefore, not its institutional framework, but its class content. According to Marx there is no such thing as a state, or therefore as a government, which has no class basis. The state comes into existence as the result of class antagonisms and is the instrument through which one class establishes its predominance. The first criterion of democracy is that it should establish the predominance of the largest class—the class which, by coming into power, automatically sweeps away all other classes and thus ushers in the classless society—the mass of the workers.

Democracy in capitalist countries [said Stalin in his speech introducing the 1936 constitution] where there are antagonistic classes is in the last analysis democracy for the strong, democracy for the propertied classes. In the U.S.S.R. on the contrary, democracy is democracy for the working people, i.e. democracy for all.

Through what constitutional forms democracy achieves this result thus becomes a subsidiary question. The overthrow of feudalism and the victory of *bourgeois* democracy in England and in France could never have been achieved except by way of the Cromwellian and Jacobin dictatorships. Marx believed, and Soviet practice has been inspired by this belief, that the only effective instrument for the overthrow of the *bourgeois* regime and the achievement of proletarian democracy would be the dictatorship of the proletariat. There is therefore no essential incompatibility between democracy and dictatorship. No doubt when the last vestiges of *bourgeois* society have been eliminated, the dictatorship of the proletariat will no longer have any purpose, and will also disappear; in the meanwhile, it is the sole means through which "democratic liberties" can be secured to the masses of the workers. The challenge

11

to the west on this point may be quite simply expressed. In the western conception of democracy institutions are all-important, and the antithesis of democracy is dictatorship; in the Soviet conception class content is the first consideration, and the antithesis of democracy is aristocracy or plutocracy, i.e. the predominance of a select class. The cult of the "common man" now fashionable in English-speaking countries is perhaps a first result of the impact of Soviet democracy.

(2) The second point is a corollary of the first. In the Soviet view, western democracy, because it is primarily formal and institutional, remains exclusively political, and lacks social and economic content. Western theory admits no necessary connexion between democracy and socialism; after 1848 it was generally assumed by western democrats that the two are not even compatible. In Soviet theory, socialism is necessary to complete democracy and to make it real. The Soviet argument on this point is so familiar that it scarcely needs recapitulation. The latter half of the 19th century showed clearly that political democracy was compatible with the continued predominance of a ruling class, and that the formal equality established by democratic institutions, i.e. one man, one vote, did not pave the way, as optimistic democrats had once expected, to economic and social equality. Democracy does not break the economic stranglehold of the employer over the worker; and freedom of the press and of public assembly does not in fact mean that equal opportunity is available for the expression of all opinions. As Trotsky cogently put it:

Democracy . . . leaves the blind play of forces in the social relations of men untouched. It was against this deeper sphere of the unconscious that the October revolution was the first to raise its head.[1]

[1] Trotsky: *The History of the Russian Revolution* (English trans., one vol. edition), p. 1191.

12

The Soviet challenge has spread and quickened the realization of these shortcomings and, in so doing, has largely contributed to the recent weakening of popular faith in the democratic institutions of the western world.

(3) The third point is the most difficult of all; for it represents an attack on the citadel of English-speaking democracy —the doctrine of toleration. It brings to a head the whole current controversy between the publicists of the English-speaking world and those of the Soviet Union. British and American writers assert that democracy does not exist in the Soviet Union because dissentient opinions are not tolerated. Soviet writers assert with equal confidence that Britain and the United States are not truly democratic because they tolerate opinions hostile to democracy. When British or Americans accuse the Russians of undemocratic behaviour in Bulgaria or Roumania, the Russians reply that all they have done is to eliminate the collaborators and thus carry out the Yalta decision to "help the liberated peoples to destroy the last vestiges of nazism and fascism". On the other hand, Mr. Churchill's policy of leaving former collaborators in power in Greece and suppressing those who formed the core of resistance to nazism, or the toleration accorded in Belgium to supporters of King Leopold, were regarded by the Russians as undemocratic. While the British and American authorities invoke democracy to justify their toleration of former collaborators and quasi-fascist groups, the Russians regard such toleration as the antithesis of democracy. A single illustration puts the issue in a nutshell. While the abolition of Regulation 18B was widely regarded in Britain as a triumph for democracy, it was regarded in Russia as a setback for democracy and a triumph for the fascists.

As has already been pointed out, English-speaking democracy has its roots in the English civil war of the 17th century and has never lost its close affinity with protestantism and specifically with dissent. The religious toleration preached by protestants and dissenters was, however, a toleration of different sects all professing loyalty in different terms to the same fundamental Christian belief. Not until religion had ceased to be a factor of political importance was toleration extended to atheists—or even to Catholics. The question posed by the recent impact of Soviet democracy on the west is whether that toleration of dissentient opinions which is declared to be the essence of democracy means toleration of all dissentient opinions, even of those hostile to democracy, or whether it means toleration of dissentient opinions on specific issues among those who accept the fundamentals of democracy. This is not an academic question, and it has not yet been answered by the spokesmen of western democracy. Neither of the alternative answers is free from difficulty.

The first answer, that democracy tolerates all dissentient opinions, even those hostile to itself, requires careful scrutiny. In fact, English-speaking democracy has almost always had on its fringe some opinion which it condemned as un-English or un-American—at different periods atheism, socialism, communism and fascism have all been cast for this role—and refused to tolerate it precisely on the ground that it threatened the foundations of democratic society. If direct political persecution is avoided, this is because the social and economic reprisals which society can apply are sufficiently powerful to prevent the offenders from becoming dangerously numerous or dangerously influential. Official spokesmen have frequently defended the toleration shown to British fascists on the ground that they are so weak and discredited that no precautionary action is required against them. The implication is that even British democracy tolerates dissentient opinions only so long as they do not become dangerous to it.

14

The thesis that democracy tolerates even dissentients hostile to itself is also open to an objection of principle. It deprives democracy of any absolute moral foundation. On this thesis the function of democracy is, so to speak, to hold the ring for all opinions, to give equal opportunity to good and evil alike, and finally to award the palm to that opinion which secures a majority of votes. It is on this ground that democracy has been attacked by the Orthodox philosopher Berdyaev, once a Marxist:

> Good and evil are alike indifferent for democracy. It is tolerant because of this indifference, because it has lost faith in truth. . . . It is a complete relativism, the negation of all absolutes.[1]

The democrat who holds that democracy requires equal toleration for opinions hostile to democracy, cannot even believe in democracy as an absolute value, being bound to accept its abrogation as valid if the majority will it. It need hardly be said that the whole of this thesis is anathema to Soviet democracy, which regards the toleration shown by English-speaking democrats to fascists as a symptom of weakness and of faltering faith in democracy.

The second answer, i.e. that the toleration proper to democracy is restricted to toleration of dissentient opinion which does not strike at the roots of democracy itself, is more sensible. It leaves no division of principle on this point between western and Soviet democracy; indeed the British and American Governments as well as the Soviet Government committed themselves unequivocally to this doctrine at the Moscow, Yalta and Potsdam conferences, when they resolved that "fascism and all its emanations should be utterly destroyed"; that nazism should be "extirpated"; and that the

[1] N. Berdyaev, *The End of Our Time*, p. 174-5.

liberated peoples of Europe should be helped to "destroy the last vestiges of nazism and fascism". But the doctrine of the extirpation of fascism leads to certain conclusions which are at present reluctantly accepted in western democracies. Whether the suppression of a dissentient opinion is permissible on the ground of the danger it presents to democratic institutions depends partly on the strength of the dissent and partly on the strength of the society against which it is directed. In other words a strong and closely-knit society like Great Britain, held together by rooted habits of common thought and action, can afford to tolerate far more diversity of opinion on matters of vital political import than a weak and fissiparous society such as we find, for example, over a large part of eastern Europe— or in India, where no principle of absolute political toleration has ever been recognized by the British rulers. Toleration of dissent on a scale perfectly safe and practicable in the English-speaking democracies might easily prove fatal altogether to democracy in Roumania or Yugoslavia.

This conclusion corresponds to common observation and to the experience of the period between the wars, and suggests the danger of seeking to transfer to democracies elsewhere the peculiar and characteristic practice of the English-speaking democracies. Even western democracy may be compelled to review its traditional attitude. The belief that British and French policy in the years before 1939 was weakened by excessive toleration extended to anti-democratic groups is not confined to the Soviet Union; nor are the more recent doubts about the setting at liberty of avowed enemies of democracy such as Sir Oswald Mosley and his friends. On the other hand admission of the right of democracy to extirpate or restrain hostile opinion, inevitable though it may be, is open to obvious and easy abuse, and English-speaking democracy, in its illogical way, may well cling to the doctrine of an absolute right to toleration, if only as a salutary corrective against the opposite extreme. But this kind of compromise is hardly suitable for export. Outside the English-speaking world the doctrine of toleration for fascists in the name of democracy will become more and more difficult to commend to popular support; and the impact of Soviet opinion will be increasingly felt against it.

(4) The fourth charge on which the challenge of Soviet democracy is based, i.e. that western democracy makes no provision for the participation of the masses in administration, is a reaction against the exclusive pre-occupation of western democracy with voting at elections. In the Soviet view the struggle between parties in *bourgeois* democracy was largely unreal—shadow-boxing between groups which, whatever their superficial differences, were equally determined to maintain the private ownership of the means of production. But, apart from this ultimate unreality of the participation of the workers in the electoral struggle, the administrative machine of the *bourgeois* state remained in the firm control of the *bourgeoisie* which sedulously fostered the view that the complicated nature of the machine made it necessary to entrust all the key posts to men of highly specialized education such as is normally available in capitalist society only to the well-to-do. This picture has no doubt been somewhat modified, so far as Great Britain is concerned, in the past 30 years; but it was still mainly true when Lenin evolved the theories on which the Soviet view of democratic administration is based.

Under Socialism [wrote Lenin in 1917] much of primitive democracy will inevitably be revived. For the first time in the history of civilized nations the mass of the people will rise to

17

direct participation, not only in voting and elections, but in the everyday administration of the affairs of the nation.[1]

Lenin's numerous attacks on bureaucracy were inspired by this intense desire to draw the masses into the direct management of affairs. No doubt some of his estimates of the possibility of substituting workers in their spare time for professional bureaucrats were naively exaggerated. But the principle of encouraging the direct participation of the Soviet citizen survived and, allowing for some reaction from the first outbursts of enthusiasm, found expression in the obligation of unpaid public service for party members and trade unionists and in the work of the local soviets.

Something of the same "revival of primitive democracy" was witnessed in Great Britain during the war in the form of Home Guard activities and of locally organized A.R.P. and civil defence services. It is worth noting that these manifestations of local and informal democracy occurred under the aegis of a highly concentrated, and—necessarily in time of war—somewhat autocratic, central authority; and it may be suggested that a socialist state is better equipped to provide opportunity for, and to stimulate, such "democratic" activities than a capitalist state in time of peace. If Soviet authorities take the view that such direct participation in the running of affairs is at least as essential an attribute of democracy as voting in occasional elections, it is by no means certain that they are wrong. The broad lines of Soviet policy may be dictated from the centre. But the Soviet Union has never ignored the human element, or underestimated the extent to which the execution of any policy depends on the enthusiasm and initiative of the individual citizen; and it has shown itself as well aware as the western world of what Sir Ernest Barker has

[1] Lenin, *State and Revolution*, ch. vi.

18

described as a main function of democracy—to "enlist the effective thought of the whole community in the operation of discussion".[1] Here at any rate is a challenge of Soviet democracy to western political institutions about which western democrats will be well advised to ponder.

[1] Ernest Barker, *Reflections on Government*, p. 444.

II

THE ECONOMIC IMPACT

THE economic impact of the Soviet Union on the rest of the world may be summed up in the single word "planning". Some years ago an acute writer observed that from the point of view of "the part played by developments in the Soviet Union in influencing the course of events in other countries . . . the activities of the Communist International . . . are much less important than those of the State Planning Commission".[1] It would be tedious to record the numerous imitations all over the world, some substantial, some superficial, of the Soviet five-year plans, to recall that Nazi Germany at one time announced a four-year plan, Turkey a five-year plan and Mexico a six-year plan, or that President Roosevelt's enemies were never tired of claiming that the New Deal had been framed on a Soviet model. It is more important to trace the origins of the concept of planning, to consider how it was developed by the Soviet Union, and to show how this development has helped to shape economic thought and economic practice even in countries which have never committed themselves to a formal plan. Certainly, if "we are all planners now", this is largely the result, conscious or unconscious, of the impact of Soviet practice and Soviet achievement.

[1] John Stanfield, *Plan We Must*, p. 74.

The pedigree of planning is extraordinarily complex. If Marx was, as is sometimes supposed, the father of planning, his paternity was of an indirect and mainly negative kind. While he wrote much of the anarchy of production under capitalism, he offered no programme for the more disciplined production which socialism might be expected to bring with it. He foresaw that trade in the capitalist sense would disappear. But he threw out no guidance for a socialist system of distribution other than the naive proposition (designed perhaps to be taken symbolically rather than literally) that the workers would "receive paper cheques by means of which they withdraw from the social supply of means of consumption a share corresponding to their labour-time".[1] Three reasons may be suggested for Marx's failure to draw anything like the blue-print of a planned socialist order.

In the first place, Marx was by temperament and conviction the sworn enemy of utopianism in any form. In his early years he had engaged in vigorous polemics against the utopian socialists who entertained themselves with unreal visions of the future socialist society. In one of his last published pamphlets *The Civil War in France* he explained that the workers have "no ready-made utopias" and "no ideals to realize", and know that "they will have to pass through long struggles, through a series of historic processes, transforming circumstances and men". This "scientific", quasi-determinist belief in the transformation of society by immanent "historic processes" seems implicitly, though perhaps unconsciously, inimical to the active pursuit of planning.

Secondly, Marx applied the tools of economic analysis to the capitalist system, but apparently did not regard these tools as relevant to a prospective socialist order. In an early work he described Proudhon as "tossing about constantly

[1] Marx, *Capital*, vol. II (English trans. 1907), p. 412.

between capital and labour, between political economy and communism".[1] "Political economy" was in his mind something that belonged essentially to capitalism and would be superseded with capitalism. The familiar economic categories of value, price and profit would cease to apply in the collective society; even the labour theory of value would change its meaning.[2] But Marx had no new categories to substitute for the old ones, and had no tools of economic analysis to use once capitalism was left behind. Discussions about the functions of price and profit in a planned economy lay far ahead in the future.

Thirdly and most important, Marx was inhibited from any serious development of planning by inability to establish by whom planning in a socialist order would be done. Vigorously as he trounced the upholders of *laissez-faire*, he was himself deeply rooted in many of its underlying assumptions; and, though he based his system on the primacy of economics over politics, he still regarded them as distinct spheres. In any case the state, as the political organ, was to wither away at no distant date, and could not be the arbiter of planning in the coming order. Hence Marx was led to suppose that, while under socialism production would come "under the conscious and pre-arranged control of society",[3] society would itself be "organized as a conscious and systematic association", in which the producers themselves "would regulate the exchange of products, and place it under their own common control instead of allowing it to rule over them as a blind force".[4] While some kind of planning and direction of economic life was clearly an integral part of socialism, Marx was content to assume that these functions would be discharged not by

[1] Marx, *The Poverty of Philosophy* (English trans.), p. 166.
[2] Marx and Engels, *Works* (Russian ed.), XV, p. 273.
[3] Marx, *Capital*, vol. III (English trans.), p. 221.
[4] Marx, *Capital*, vol. III (English trans.), p. 773.

the state or by any political organ, but by the producers themselves; and beyond this he did not go.

Nor did his disciples down to 1917 make any significant progress along this line. In the fifty years which followed the publication of *Capital* no really significant contribution was made to the theoretical elaboration of a socialist economic order. "We knew when we took power into our hands," said Lenin six months after the October revolution, "that there were no ready forms of concrete reorganization of the capitalist system into a socialist one. . . . I do not know of any socialist who has dealt with these problems." And speaking of production and exchange, he added: "There was nothing written about such matters in the Bolshevik text-books, or even in those of the Mensheviks." Nothing substantial had been added to Marx's vague notion of a self-organization of the workers into communes or communities of producers.

Planning, in the sense of the central direction of a national economy towards a centrally determined end or series of ends, was a product of national emergency rather than of a desire for social reform. On the theoretical side, the title of father of planning belongs rather to Friedrich List than to Karl Marx. Not only did List's *National System of Political Economy* lay a foundation for national planning as a means of building up German industrial strength but rudiments of the process of planning are scattered here and there through his works.[1] It was the war of 1914–18 which taught the les-

[1] In a pamphlet significantly entitled *On a Saxon Railway System as Foundation of a General German Railway System*, List, writing in 1833, used an argument fundamental to planning which would have come pat a century later:

"What is an expenditure of 4 millions, yes, I ask, what is an expenditure of 6 or 10 millions, where such great national interests are at stake, and where at the same time the capital invested earns such extraordinarily high interest? The more capital that can be invested in such conditions the better. The mere investment of such large capital sums spreads food, work, happi-

23

son that the most efficient organization of production for a socially necessary purpose could not be achieved within the limits of the free capitalist system, that is to say, through the stimulus of the price mechanism, and that direct control and organization of production by the state was required. The lesson was learned scarcely at all in Russia, and at best partially in Great Britain. It was learned thoroughly only in the fatherland of List where the name of "planned economy" was invented, and its practice developed, by Rathenau and his experts in the German War Raw Materials Department. Thus, except in the limited sense that a community at war has a stronger incentive than at any other time to prevent the growth of resentments due to inequality of conditions or of sacrifices, and necessarily accepts in some degree the principle of distribution "to each according to his needs", planned economy in its first developed form owed nothing to ideals of socialism or social justice.

The first approach to planning in Soviet Russia was extremely tentative and hesitant. The process of "nationalization" meant, in the early days of the revolution, the taking over of the factories by the workers, of the land by those who tilled it. "Every factory and every farm", said Lenin in 1918, would constitute "a production and consumption commune" and would "solve in its own way the problem of calculating the production and distribution of products". There is little evidence to show how far the Bolshevik leaders were alive to . the implications of planned economy in war-time Germany; but it was war—this time civil war—which also imposed the elements of planning on Soviet Russia. In Russia, as in Germany, national survival depended on the organization of limited national resources as a single whole in which each part

ness and well-being among the masses of the population along the line, since nine-tenths of the expenditure benefit the working class."

was controlled or directed towards the fulfilment of a national aim. This was the period of "war communism" whose horrors and hardships afterwards gave it a bad name in Soviet history. But, in the Soviet Union as elsewhere, a certain military aroma clung to the terminology of planning: there continued to be agrarian and industrial "fronts", "battles" of production, "shock brigades" of workers and so forth.

It was the experience of these years, combined with the intuition of Lenin, which really started "planning" on its world-wide career. Lenin and his coadjutors clearly perceived that victory in the civil war would be the beginning not the end of the difficulties of the regime. Neither national security in a hostile world, nor the survival of the proletarian revolution at home, could be hoped for without a policy of intensive industrialization. Since foreign capital in any significant amount was unobtainable, the capital required could be provided only by exploitation of the peasant mass; and this exploitation would be wholly intolerable if it were not mitigated by a rise in the efficiency and productivity of Soviet agriculture. The necessary increase of productivity could, Lenin thought, be achieved through a plan for the wholesale extension of electric power throughout the Russian countryside; and in December 1920, immediately at the end of the civil war, a state commission was appointed to elaborate such a plan. The idea was a mixture of naivety and brilliance. The fundamental conception was profoundly right; the details were often utopian. Perhaps the most important fact about the project was that it was thought of merely as the first of a number of plans through which productivity could be increased by a deliberate and centrally directed reorganization of the national economy. But this was not yet planning in the sense of a balanced and integrated direction of the whole national economy: it was simply a collection of separate plans for the fulfilment of particular objects or the rehabilitation of particular industries. The Soviet Union eventually reached global planning through the stage of a number of partial and unco-ordinated plans.

The period of the New Economic Policy (NEP) was a period of struggle and contradiction between, on the one hand, the need to make the economy work by appeasing the peasant and, on the other hand, the desire to build up a strong national economy on socialist lines at any cost short of a complete breakdown. The significant decisions which prepared the way for the victory of planning were those of the thirteenth Party Congress in favour of "socialism in one country" and of the fourteenth Congress in favour of "industrialization". Neither of these could be achieved through the operations of a "free" economy; and from the moment when they were adopted, NEP became obsolete and began to wither away. In 1925 the first "control figures" (a sort of industrial budget)—for the year 1925–6—were produced. In 1927 the first tentative five-year plan, under the title *Control Figures for the Industry of the USSR for the Five Years 1927–8 to 1931–2*, was submitted to the fifteenth Party Congress. The official first Five-Year Plan came into effect on October 1, 1928. This date marked the final liquidation of NEP and the adhesion of the Soviet Union to a policy of planning which has been vigorously pursued ever since. It is in a sense true that both "war communism" and NEP had been forced responses to national emergencies. The period of the Five-Year Plans represented the first voluntary and deliberate adoption by the Soviet Union of the policy of planning.

.   .   .   .   .

This complicated ancestry of planning in the Soviet Union, and of planning in general, makes it curiously difficult to an-

26

swer in clear or concise terms the question, Why plan? or, What are we planning for? The answer is two-fold. Planning is a Janus-like affair having both a national and a social face. It stands for national efficiency in the sense of more efficient production and it stands for social justice in the sense of more equitable distribution, the link between the two aspects being a deliberate rejection of, and reaction from, the *laissez-faire* thesis that efficiency in production and justice in distribution will both be most nearly assured by a system which allows the least public interference with the automatic operation of the economic order. We need not at this moment consider which aspect of planning historically or logically precedes the other. Both are necessary. If we neglect the "national" aspect, we shall forget that planning is required just as much for national efficiency in production as for social justice in distribution; and we may then fall into the error of those socialists who believe that, once wealth and incomes have been equalized in obedience to the claims of social justice, the direction of production into the required channels can be left under socialism, as in a *laissez-faire* economy, to the uninhibited working of the price mechanism. If on the other hand we neglect the "social" aspect, we shall fall into the heresy of efficiency for efficiency's sake and conclude that planning is simply the instrument of national power and national aggrandisement—the doctrine of fascism. Hitlerism took the name of national socialism. But the fact that it was not capitalist did not make it socialist: it approximated far more nearly to the conceptions of the American "technocrats" or of Mr. Burnham's "managerial revolution"—the cult of efficiency for the sake of power. The Soviet Union has been generally accepted as the creator of contemporary "planning", not so much because it first started planning or

27

even because it did it more thoroughly than anyone else, but because it has most successfully combined the national and social aspects of planning into a single policy.

The essence of planning in its national aspect is the treatment of the nation as an economic unit and its substitution for the accidental unit of corporation, firm or individual trader. It should be noted at this point that there is no logical reason why planning should stop at the nation. In theory the sequel to national planning is international planning, and some reference will be made to this in a later chapter. But for the moment the nation remains in general the largest effective planning unit.

The first thing to note about the national aspect of planning is that it is a continuation and development of processes already set in motion under capitalism. Ever since producers and traders began to get together and form groups, companies and associations for the furtherance of their interests in common, there has been planning of a kind. The development of capitalism, following the lines of the struggle for life and the survival of the fittest in accordance with the purest *laissez-faire* principles, led to the formation of more and more comprehensive and powerful groups: the units by and for which plans were made grew larger. No point was in sight—certainly no point short of the national community—at which this development would naturally be halted. Capitalism itself had paved the way for planning on a national scale and made it logical and inevitable. Rathenau is reported to have said that he had learned all he knew about planned economy from his father, the creator and managing director of the A.E.G. "The true pacemakers of socialism", a recent writer has said, "were not the intellectuals or agitators who preached it, but the Vanderbilts, Carnegies and Rockefellers".[1] Things had

[1] J. A. Schumpeter, *Capitalism, Socialism and Democracy*, p. 134.

reached the point, foreseen by Marx in a famous passage of *Capital*, at which "centralization of the means of production and socialization of labour at last . . . become incompatible with their capitalist integument." As Lenin wrote:

> Compulsory syndicalization, i.e. compulsory unification into associations under state control, that is what capitalism has prepared, that is what the *junker* state has carried out in Germany, that is what will be fully carried out in Russia for the Soviets, for the dictatorship of the proletariat.[1]

Capitalism is progressive, Lenin had written earlier, so long as it is developing the forces of production; but "all the same, at a certain stage of development, it holds up the growth of productive forces".[2] Capitalism becomes reactionary and seeks to arrest the natural process of its own development when it opposes planning by and for the national unit.

The question here arises why this point should have been reached first of all in industrially backward Russia, and why therefore the Soviet Union should have led the world in national planning. The superficial answer, valid as far as it goes, is that planning has more immediate attractions for poor countries than for rich ones. The essence of planning is the considered assignment of priorities for the allocation of scarce resources. A man earning £5 a week has, other things being equal, more cause to plan than a man with £5,000 a year. Nations take more readily to planning in times of war or economic crisis than in the palmy days of peace and prosperity. Great Britain, as she has grown poorer, has recognized more clearly the need to plan. The richest country in the world today is the most recalcitrant to planning. Hence it is not unnatural that Russia, the poorest and most backward of

---

[1] Lenin, *Works*, XXI (in Russian), pp. 261-2.
[2] Lenin, *Works*, XV (in Russian), p. 6.

the great modern nations, should have been a pioneer of planning. Russian planners, from Peter to Stalin, have repeatedly justified their policy by the need of enabling backward Russia to catch up with the more advanced European nations.

The more profound reason why the Soviet Union has led the way in planning is that Russia was industrially backward only in the sense that Russian industry occupied a relatively insignificant proportion of the population and was not particularly efficient. In another sense it was anything but backward. In Russia, capitalism, having been imported from abroad and not developed from individual craftsmanship by a slow, indigenous growth, had from the first been large-scale capitalism; and much of it had from the first worked in close dependence on the state. Except for the textile industry, industrialization in Russia was not primarily inspired, as it had been in western Europe, by entrepreneurs in search of profits. It was directly fostered and supported by the state, mainly in the interests of military efficiency. At the moment of the introduction of the first Five-Year Plan, Stalin appropriately recalled how "Peter the Great, having to deal with the more developed countries of the west, feverishly built factories and workshops to supply the army and strengthen the defence of the country".[1] In the closing years of the 19th century the introduction into Russia of modern heavy industry was promoted by the Finance Minister, Witte, and financed by French capitalists, mainly in the interests of Russian military preparedness. Thus in its predilection for large-scale organization, in its dependence on state initiative and patronage, and in the absence of serious opposition from smaller private capitalism (the principal enemy of planning in western Europe), the Russian economic system, in spite of its backwardness in

[1] Stalin, *Leninism*, II, p. 153.

other respects, was particularly well adapted to become the pioneer of national planning.

Planning is therefore in one aspect simply a culmination of the long process of development which successively replaced the individual craftsman or trader by the small business, the small business by the large company, and the large company by the giant combine, so that the national economic unit is merely the greatest combine of all—a vast agglomeration of associated, affiliated and subsidiary companies or enterprises of all shapes and sizes, pursuing the same general policy under the same general direction at the centre. This view will throw immediate light on some of the problems of planning; for many of the difficulties of policy and accountancy now being faced on the national plane have been met and solved for years past by the management of large industrial or commercial concerns. It has long been a commonplace that it will pay a large firm to sell a product for a considerable period at a loss in order to build up a market for it, bearing the loss on the rest of the firm's turn-over: this in the national sphere is the well-worn "infant industry" argument for protection. It is a commonplace that, once a market has been established for a product at a price which leaves a satisfactory margin over cost, it may pay to find fresh outlets for an expansion of production at a lower price—even at a price below average costs—so long as the higher price markets are not thereby affected: this in the sphere of international trade is what is called dumping. It is a commonplace that a large firm will desire to make sure of essential supplies of raw materials or other components by long-term and often exclusive contracts with suppliers: these are known internationally as bulk purchase agreements. It may even create subsidiary companies to produce under its own supervision what it requires: these are known internationally as "spheres of influence" or "concessions". But there is another parallel of a rather different kind. No firm, however large or however small, can for any length of time afford to keep idle hands. Once the nation becomes the economic unit it cannot tolerate idle workers. Planning makes nonsense of unemployment.

Planning therefore for the national unit for the first time entails a view of the national economy as a whole. *Laissez-faire* was justified, and could only be justified, on the assumption that individuals working separately in their own interest contrived without intending it to achieve the highest good of the community—the famous doctrine of the natural harmony of interests. We know that, for a variety of reasons, this assumption was never fully valid and that it has long lost the limited degree of validity which it once possessed. Planning presupposes that the interest of the community has to be predetermined by a decision in the formulation of which individuals and their interests play a part, though governmental authority is required to bring them into harmony. Hence government is now concerned with the whole national economy. The traditional state "budget" covered, and still covers, only that part of the national income which is for one reason or another directly handled by the administrative organs of the state; and under a regime of planning it is often a matter of policy, almost of accident, whether particular items figure in the budget or are excluded from it. Nor is there any particular reason why the budget in the old sense should not show a deficit and why this deficit should not persist indefinitely. The framing of the budget involves the minor decision how much the nation can afford to devote to the maintenance of "non-productive" services—administrative, social, cultural and so forth; it involves the further, and also minor, decision how far these services should be financed by fees collected from the beneficiaries, by taxation, or by borrowing, i.e. by a deficit which must be made good out of other sectors of the national economy. But the drawing up of the comprehensive national economic plan, the division of productive resources between production for consumption and production for capital accumulation, the fixing of wage levels and price levels, the framing of currency and credit policy—all these major decisions fall outside its scope. These are the decisions which in the Soviet Union since 1928 have been incorporated in the Five-Year Plans—the real budgets of the whole national economy. In Great Britain, it is only since 1941 that the Central Statistical Office attached to the Cabinet Secretariat has issued an annual estimate of "National Income and Expenditure" which has gradually come to eclipse the traditional budget in importance. Devised as a war expedient this annual White Paper has quickly become a national institution, and the necessary foundation of any national investment and full employment policy. Thus Great Britain, following the Soviet precedent, has, not yet, it is true, a full-grown national plan, but at any rate the basic statistical material on which any such plan must be founded. At last there is unequivocal recognition that what really matters is not what the government as such spends and receives but what the community as a whole consumes and produces.

.   .   .   .   .

But what have we learned, or can we learn, from Soviet precept or practice about the methods and instruments of national planning? Lord Keynes once confessed in a rash moment that he could not "perceive that Russian communism has made any contribution to our economic problems of intellectual interest or scientific value".[1] Nevertheless, even if it were demonstrated—as I think it can be—that Lord Keynes

[1] J. M. Keynes, *A Short View of Russia* (1925), reprinted in *Essays in Persuasion* (1931), p. 306.

reached his own conclusions by different routes and quite independently of anything that happened in Russia, it would be still true to say that the main positions of "Keynesian economics" had already been established in Soviet economic policies, and that Lord Keynes's doctrines found such ready acceptance in Great Britain and elsewhere partly because the ground had already been prepared in the minds of his contemporaries by contemplation of the planned economy of the Soviet Union.

The cardinal positions of the Keynesian economic revolution may be summarized as follows:—

(*a*) that resources left unused owing to individual abstinence from consumption do not necessarily, or by any automatic process, find their way into "investment", i.e. the creation of productive capital.

(*b*) that abstinence of the well-to-do from consumption, far from being an unconditional blessing, may be less useful to the community than their spending, and that the classical argument which justifies inequality of wealth as an impetus to investment thus disappears. (Lord Keynes at one time looked forward with satisfaction to "the euthanasia of the *rentier*".)

(*c*) that, even in default of a sufficient volume of individual savings and investment, investment can still be maintained at the requisite level by "communal saving through the agency of the state", i.e. through fiscal policy.

(*d*) that this "communal saving", together with its counterpart the "comprehensive socialization of investment", i.e. the treatment of investment not as an automatic product of private savings in search of profit, but as a decision of public policy, is the condition of full employment.

It would not be difficult to show that these principles had been applied in the Soviet Union and accepted as the basis of Soviet planning before they were worked out in the form of economic theory by Lord Keynes. The elimination of the *rentier*

34

in Soviet Russia, by a process perhaps less humane than that contemplated in Lord Keynes's aphorism, deprived Soviet planners of any temptation to rely on voluntary private savings, or voluntary abstinence from consumption, for the creation of the capital necessary for industrialization; nor could they resort to the process of borrowing foreign capital by which the nations of the new world had built up their industries. They were therefore driven by force of circumstances rather than by economic argument to Lord Keynes's conclusion that the full employment of their resources could only be achieved, first, by "communal saving through the agency of the state", which was achieved partly by direct and indirect taxation, partly by compulsory borrowing, supported by rationing and price-fixing policies, and, secondly, by that "comprehensive socialization of investment" which is the essence of planning.

The main task of planning is the establishment of priorities for the investment of national resources, including in that term both materials and man-power; and since this means the allocation of scarce resources among a larger number of purposes than can possibly all be attained, consistent planning can leave no room—except, of course, through some temporary dislocation—for unused resources or unemployed man-power. No frontal attack on unemployment, such as was continually under discussion in the 'thirties throughout the western world, was ever made in the Soviet Union. It was indeed a grave problem in the Soviet Union of the later 'twenties, and was recognized as such. But it was rightly treated not as substantive evil, but as the symptom of a diseased economy. It was attributed to the capitalist elements in NEP and was automatically absorbed by the first Five-Year Plan. In other words full employment was achieved, as it always should be, not as an end in itself, but as the by-product of a determination to fulfil other purposes. What is of interest, and what has made so profound an impression on the outside world, is a consideration of the means by which full employment was effected.

The initial and fundamental choice in planning must be to settle the proportion of production for consumption and production for capital accumulation respectively.[1] Until this point is reached, i.e. until a national investment policy has been worked out, there can be no real planning. Now although resources left unused through abstinence from consumption do not automatically flow into investment for capital accumulation, it is nevertheless true that in conditions of full employment the decision to invest for capital accumulation imposes *pro tanto* a reduction of consumption. In a rich and highly industrialized economy the rate of investment for capital accumulation (renewal and development of machinery, equipment, etc.) tends to lag behind the capacity for voluntary saving, so that its effect on consumption will not be ordinarily noticed. But in a country undergoing either a rapid process of industrialization or any other radical transformation of its economy, the rate of capital accumulation may have to be raised so sharply as to impose a conspicuous reduction of consumption; and this condition approximates to that of a country at war where a similar reduction of consumption is imposed by the need to invest all available resources in the output of non-productive armaments. It is for this reason that the planning policies of the Soviet Union provide so many precedents for British practice during the second world war. For the same reason these precedents will remain valid during

[1] Marx himself had written that under socialism "society must calculate beforehand how much labour, means of production and means of subsistence it can utilize without injury for such lines of activity as, for instance, the building of railroads." (*Capital*, vol. II. (English trans. 1907), p. 361).

the period of radical economic re-adjustment which confronts Great Britain after the war. The explanatory White Paper issued with the Bill to create a National Investment Council stated clearly that

it is the policy of His Majesty's Government to establish and maintain a proper balance between the economic resources of the community and the demands upon them. This means that priority must always be assured for those projects of capital development which are of the greatest importance in the national interest.[1]

The "socialization of investment", carrying with it a considered choice between production for consumption and production for capital accumulation, runs through the whole history of Soviet planning. Industrialization in the oversea countries, as well as in some parts of western Europe, had been effected largely on borrowed capital. Great Britain was intensively industrialized without borrowing in the early years of the 19th century through the ruthless exploitation of a working population driven by various pressures from the country into the towns. But Great Britain was already at the time a highly developed community, possessing a large and vigorous middle class, a productive agriculture and a nucleus of individual craftsmen and small workshops busily engaged on the output of consumers' goods. Russia had none of these things; and the Soviet planners, once the slack of unemployment in the later 1920's had been taken up, had no resource but to procure the capital for industrialization by imposing a forced abstention from consumption on a mainly peasant population living at, or sometimes below, a bare subsistence level. The constant dilemma of Soviet planning policy was to impose on a predominantly peasant population a degree of abstention from consumption sufficient to finance industrial-

[1] Cmd. 6726, p. 2.

ization without provoking either a refusal on the part of the peasants to produce food to supply the industrial worker or a refusal on the part of the industrial workers to man the factories for wages which represented a restricted and inadequate purchasing power.

Russian conditions do not therefore provide a precise precedent for planning in countries where the main task of industrialization has been achieved and relatively high standards of living attained. But the principle of the choice between production for immediate consumption and production for accumulation is essential to all planning; and many of the devices adopted in Britain during the war—some of them likely to be perpetuated—were the inventions of Soviet planners. Thus rationing in order to secure the equitable distribution of consumption goods which cannot be produced in sufficient quantity to meet demand has been combined with differential rationing designed to stimulate production among factory workers. One such differential device, the well-supplied factory canteen, was widely used in Britain during the war; another, the cheap factory shop, has not appeared in Britain, but may yet come. The vodka monopoly, abolished after the 1917 revolution, was restored in the Soviet Union in 1924 in order to drain off purchasing power into a commodity whose production costs were low and a large proportion of whose high sale price returned at once to the exchequer in the form of taxation—the policy now pursued in Great Britain with tobacco and beer. Since Britain will be faced for some time to come with the dilemma of needing to increase productivity while being at the same time unable to provide consumption goods in sufficient abundance to satisfy available purchasing power, the adoption of more of the devices of Soviet planners may be safely predicted. Privileged housing for industrial and other essential workers has been a feature

38

of the Russian economy and is a probability of the near future elsewhere.

The "socialization of investment" provides the answer to another fundamental difficulty of modern capitalism, the problem of risk-taking. The notion that the needs of technical progress can be assured and the requisite degree of inventiveness fostered by the prospect of high profits accruing to the ingenious inventor, or to the bold entrepreneur who invests his capital in the invention, became obsolete with the demise of the small business. In the days of "imperfect competition" and quasi-monopoly, of big combines and of enormous investments in fixed plant, the vastness of the investment required to develop and exploit any important invention is itself sufficient to explain why capital has become less adventurous. The contemporary speculator generally prefers to gamble in produce or in stocks and shares rather than to found new enterprises. This leaves technical progress and invention to the mercy of giant combines whose resources are so vast as virtually to eliminate the notion of risk. But there is no guarantee that the considerations which move a large concern to undertake research, or to exploit an invention, are those which, on a still broader view, would seem technically or socially decisive. As a matter of fact, many of the great inventions of the present age have been exploited for the first time under the impact of war, when considerations of profit and loss have become altogether inoperative. The western countries at present occupy a half-way position. The notion of adventurous private capital taking risks in search of high profits and thus promoting technical progress is virtually dead. The notion that investment for this purpose should be determined by social ends, using the term in its broadest sense, has not yet won widespread acceptance outside the Soviet Union. But there is no doubt that this is the direction in which the

39

western world, partly under the influence of Soviet example, is steadily moving.

Since the price-fixing policies of the western countries are in a similar intermediate position, it may be appropriate to add a few reflexions on the functions of currency and prices in a planned economy, and on the lessons which can be learned from Soviet planning on this point. The conception of a managed currency did not originate in the Soviet Union. Shortly after the first world war the notion of a currency geared not to gold or any fixed standard, but to a variable price index, was canvassed by many economists, including Professor Irving Fisher in the United States and Lord Keynes in Great Britain. A further elaboration of this idea was Gustav Cassel's proposal for "purchasing power parity" as a regulator of foreign exchanges, so that currencies would fluctuate internationally in conformity with price levels. The assumption behind all these proposals was that prices were "naturally" determined, and that, while currencies could with advantage be "managed", prices would be left unmanaged.

The Soviet authorities themselves experimented with this theory in the early 1920's. In 1921, faced with the impossibility of any kind of budgeting in progressively depreciating roubles, they decided that the budget should be drawn up in terms of 1913 roubles with a shifting rate of conversion into current roubles on the basis of a monthly price index. This system disappeared with the stabilization of the currency in 1924; and with the introduction of planning it became clear that "managed" prices were as much part of a planned economy as a "managed" currency and that neither one nor the other could be the basis of a fixed standard. In 1931—about the time when Great Britain began to experiment with a currency based on price stabilization—the Soviet Government discovered that a price index is meaningless in a planned economy and ceased to issue one. Not till the second world war did Great Britain resort on an extensive scale to a policy of "managed" prices, with the tentative beginnings of a policy of differential prices for different categories of the population. It seems safe to predict that in Great Britain, as in the Soviet Union, price-fixing will remain an important instrument of social policy in a planned economy, and that the price index will become more and more unreal as a guide to economic policy.

Having come thus far, we are faced with the question where to find our ultimate standard of value, our test of efficiency. If not in currencies, if not in commodity prices, where? And the answer can only be found in some set of values determined by a consciously adopted social policy. The argument thus brings us back from the national to the social aspect of planning. Planning, in fact, automatically raises a number of questions which cannot be answered on grounds of abstract efficiency and depend on an answer to the previous question, Planning for what? or, Efficiency for what? What proportion of available resources should be devoted to the production of consumer and capital goods respectively? Within these categories, how should priorities be determined for the production of particular commodities? What consideration should govern price-fixing policies? What "profit" margins should be allowed for, and how should "profits" be distributed? In war, these questions answer themselves. Planning is essential to national survival and for this purpose almost any sacrifice is worth while. In peace, planning can be maintained only if it is directed to social purposes sufficiently strong to provide an accepted standard of values and to claim loyalty and self-sacrifice from its citizens for their attainment. The achievement of the Soviet Union has been to establish planning as a normal peace-time procedure and as the instrument of a social policy carrying with it both rights and obligations for the citizen.

III

THE SOCIAL IMPACT

IT IS interesting to reflect why the 20th century has been so much more concerned than its predecessor with social policies. Economically, this is due, as was suggested in the last chapter, to the need for planning which presupposes a social policy. Sociologically, it is explained by the increase in numbers and influence of an organized working class, concentrated in factories and cities—the product of industrial civilization. Ideologically, it is the decay of the negative doctrine of *laissez-faire* which has called for a new and positive social philosophy. The *laissez-faire* ideology which predominated in the 19th century encouraged the belief that the interplay of individuals each pursuing his own rational interest automatically produced the best social results, and that the proper function of government was to maintain order and fair play among competing individuals, but not to initiate an active social policy. Hence no definition of social purposes was required. Orthodox opinion tended to believe that governments were a necessary evil and that the less positive action they took, the better. But under the pressure of industrial conditions, and the growth of working-class parties imbued with socialist doctrine, this opinion had begun to wear thin by the first decade of the 20th century. Today it has hardly any wholehearted adherents left, except perhaps in certain circles in the United States. The case for a greater or smaller degree of social planning is now almost universally accepted; and in this retreat from *laissez-faire* Soviet example has been a predominant influence.

So far as the western world is concerned, however, the retreat has been only partial; the battle-ground has merely shifted. On the one hand, the residuary legatees of *laissez-faire* argue nowadays not indeed that state intervention is always and in all circumstances to be deprecated, but that it should be undertaken piecemeal, to meet urgent needs or remedy glaring injustices. On the other hand, the planners demand a coherent and considered social and economic policy extending to almost every field of public affairs to promote both national efficiency and social justice. The reluctance of the western nations to adopt planning on a comprehensive scale is partly connected with their traditionally empirical habits of thought, their reluctance to formulate a comprehensive social philosophy. Yet once the automatism of *laissez-faire* is abandoned, the decisions inherent in planning can only be taken, implicitly or explicitly, on the basis of such a philosophy.

Soviet planning is directed, as all coherent planning must be, to the fulfilment of defined social purposes. In words once used by Trotsky, "the Soviet system wishes to bring aim and plan into the very basis of society".[1] Three fundamental points underlie the social philosophy of Soviet planning. In the first place, it combines a material and a moral appeal. Secondly, it is defined not in individual, but in social or collective terms. Thirdly, it demands a recognition of equal social obligations as well as of equal social rights.

The material purpose of the social philosophy of planning is the aim avowed by socialism from the outset and defined

[1] Trotsky, *The History of the Russian Revolution* (English trans., one vol. edition), p. 1191.

43

more than a century ago by Saint-Simon—"to improve as much as possible the lot of the class which has no other means of existence but the labour of its hands".[1] This was the starting-point of Marx. The avowed social purpose of Soviet planning is to improve the lot of the common man, and, in particular, to raise his standard of living. As long ago as 1870 the *bourgeois* historian Burckhardt noted "the desire of the masses for a higher standard of living" as "the dominating feeling of our age";[2] and Marxism has encouraged the now commonly accepted belief that improved material standards of living are the foundation of other forms of improvement. Nevertheless it would be a mistake to suppose that the goal of planning is conceived in purely material terms. The attention given to education and cultural activities does not suggest a narrowly materialist view of the task of improving the lot of the workers; and the degree of moral fervour for the social purposes of Soviet policy which is, according to all observers, generated among the citizens of the Soviet Union is an answer to those critics who used to argue that Marxism could never be successful because it lacked a moral appeal.

The moral appeal is strongly reinforced by the demand, implicit in Soviet ideology, for social justice in the form of equality between man and man. The equality preached in the Soviet Union is not an equality of function or an equality of reward. Socially important functions discharged or socially important work done are legitimate and relevant grounds for inequality. But equality, in the sense in which it is one of the fundamental purposes of Soviet social policy, means non-discrimination between human beings on irrelevant grounds such as sex, race, colour or class. Soviet principles and practice compare favourably in this respect with those of some

[1] Weill, *Saint-Simon et les Saint-Simoniens*, p. 175.
[2] J. Burckhardt, *Reflections on History* (English trans.), p. 203.

44

democratic countries. One effect of the Soviet impact on these countries has been an increased recognition of the irrelevance of such barriers and a strengthened demand to sweep them away.

Secondly, the social purpose which governs Soviet policy and Soviet planning is defined in terms not of individual demand, but of social need. The conception of planning implies that society has the right and the obligation to decide by a collective act what is good for the society as a whole and to make that decision binding on the individual. Politically, this has always been admitted. Economically, the philosophy of *laissez-faire* was exclusively individualist. It recognized no good which could not be measured in terms of individual demand, the social good being merely the automatic by-product of an uninhibited interplay of individual interests. Old-fashioned economists like Professor von Mises and Professor von Hayek, who still accept this philosophy, argue that there can be no such thing as a social purpose and that all planning must be arbitrary and irrational. This is partly a matter of terminology. If measurable individual demand is the sole rational criterion of the "greatest good of the greatest number", then planning remains in this sense "irrational". But it is a curiously defeatist view of human nature, and fails altogether to tally with the facts, to hold that the only social good which can be recognized as rational is the victory of one's nation in war, and that it is impossible to define rationally any other social purpose for which the individual can properly be asked to sacrifice himself. Naturally the pursuit of any social purpose, like any other human activity, is likely to be tainted by individual interest, and the process of planning for its fulfilment, like every other function of government, may involve acts of individual oppression. But it seems pointless to deny that men and women in their social and economic activities formulate purposes

45

which cannot be measured in terms of individual demand, and are as ready to sacrifice themselves in the pursuit of those purposes as they are in the pursuit of individual interest. The essential difference between *laissez-faire* and socialism in all its manifold shapes is that socialism explicitly recognizes the existence of collective social purposes and the ultimate right of society to give an authoritative definition of them. "To each according to his needs" implies a judgment by society of what the needs of the individual are. Such a judgment provides the rational basis for the priorities established by planning. Admittedly it implies decisions of public policy in a field from which public action was excluded by the doctrine of *laissez-faire*. But this is the essence of planning. The retort "Who will plan the planners?" is no more than a smart debating-point; it merely registers the fundamental dilemma of all government that authority is a necessary condition of any social order and that all authority is liable to be abused.

Thirdly, the social purpose of the Soviet system demands a recognition of equal social obligations as well as of equal social rights. As the driving force of the economic system, it attempts to substitute the positive incentive of social obligation for the negative incentive of the fear of penury and hunger. The issue provokes acute controversy, the basis of which is emotional rather than rational. The western world— workers as well as capitalists—has generally been disposed to think that the indirect impersonal pressure of need is a less objectionable way of driving men to work than the direct compulsion of a public authority. In theory, at any rate, the indirect method seems to offer the worker greater freedom in the choice of a job, though where jobs are scarce this freedom is more theoretical than real. The Soviet view has consistently been that nothing can be more degrading to the worker than the constraint imposed on him by the capitalist

46

employer who exploits him for personal profit; since there must be some form of discipline for the individual worker, the most honourable compulsion is that imposed directly by a public authority representing the will and the interests of the whole body of the workers.

It would be rash to suggest that such views have yet been widely accepted, or even understood, in the west. But how far the climate of opinion has changed even in Great Britain is shown by an utterance of that staunch trade unionist—certainly no ardent champion of the Soviet Union—Mr. Bevin, who in a speech in the House of Commons as Minister of Labour, spoke of the difficulty of explaining the Essential Works Order to "people who never expected to have discipline of any kind except the most unfortunate discipline of all, the economic whip", and added that "you cannot have social security in this country without having some obligation".[1] In Russia the obligation of the individual to serve the state in whatever capacity the state might direct was firmly established by Peter the Great, if not earlier. The institution of serfdom survived till 1861. Until that time, the obligation to work rested, for the vast majority of Russian workers, on legal status. Only thereafter was legal compulsion replaced in Russia, as in western Europe, by the "economic whip"; and it may be doubted whether the change seemed as significant to most of those affected as it did to historians and publicists. Certainly in Russia there was likely to be less opposition than in the west to the re-establishment of a direct legal obligation to work.

.   .   .   .   .

The development of Soviet policy in regard to labour makes an instructive study. "The right to work" was a slogan dating

[1] *Parliamentary Debates: House of Commons*, 5 vols., 380 (May 21, 1942), col. 423.

47

from the 1840's: it was the natural socialist answer to the capitalist doctrine of the need for "a reserve army of labour". But socialists soon began to realize that the right to work under capitalism would have to be transformed into an obligation to work under socialism. As early as May 1917, Lenin introduced into Bolshevik propaganda the idea of a general obligation to work, and this was endorsed by a resolution of the Party Congress in July 1917. In his famous pamphlet, *Will the Bolsheviks Be Able to Retain Power?*, written on the eve of the Bolshevik revolution, Lenin quoted for the first time "He that does not work neither shall he eat", and added:

This is the fundamental, primary rule which the Soviets of Workers' Deputies can and will introduce as soon as they assume power.[1]

The "Declaration of the Rights of the Toiling and Exploited People" issued by the All-Russian Congress of Soviets in January 1918 asserted the general obligation to work. This was repeated in the first constitution of the Russian Socialist Federal Soviet Republic adopted later in the same year; and the constitution of the Soviet Union of 1936 follows Lenin in quoting "He that does not work neither shall he eat"— probably the only biblical text which has figured in a Soviet official document.

At first, the principle of the obligation to work was enunciated as if it were a weapon aimed against the idle rich. It was introduced, according to the Declaration of January 1918, "for the purpose of abolishing the parasitic strata of society and of organizing economic life". But the revolution, in wiping out this not very numerous class, soon changed the application of the principle.

[1] Lenin, *Works*, XXI (in Russian), p. 263.

48

In a system of state capitalism [as Bukharin put it] universal obligation to work is the enslavement of the working masses; in a system of proletarian dictatorship it is simply the self-organization of the masses for work.[1]

The first weeks of the revolution brought a general decay of discipline in the factories and a drifting away of the workers; and it soon became a condition not merely of economic well-being but of bare survival that this process should be arrested. At the session of the Supreme Economic Council in March 1918 the Vice-President of the Council, Milyutin, spoke in tentative language of the necessity of

labour direction in the broad sense of the term, not labour direction as it has been enforced in the west, not labour direction in the sense imagined by the masses, i.e. that all must be put to work, but labour direction as a system of the discipline of labour and as a system of the organization of labour in the interests of production.

Milyutin, who was one of the earliest advocates of planning, went on to argue that no planning of production was possible without "the establishment of a norm of definite obligatory work", and added that this could be based "only on the independence and iron self-discipline of the masses of the workers".[2] This is probably the first explicit recognition on record of the fact, which is still not everywhere fully accepted, that planning requires some "system of the organization of labour in the interests of production".

Even in Soviet Russia it might have taken some time to push this argument to its conclusion but for the outbreak of civil war and foreign intervention, which began in the summer

[1] Bukharin, *Ekonomika Perekhodnogo Perioda*, Part I (Moscow 1920), p. 109.
[2] V. P. Milyutin, *Istoriya Ekonomicheskogo Razvitiya SSSR*, p. 137–8.

of 1918. For two and a half years the new regime was fighting for its life, and any form of mobilization was accepted as a national necessity. Exactly how much was achieved cannot be guessed: this was a period of utmost confusion and of laws and decrees issued in haste with little regard to the possibility of enforcing them. After a spate of laws, decrees and resolutions proclaiming a universal obligation to work, a committee on universal compulsory labour was set up in February 1920 under the presidency of Dzerzhinsky, and a specific decree was issued calling up three "classes" for labour service in September 1920. The name of Trotsky is especially associated with the organization of "labour battalions". His trenchant mind, untrammelled by considerations of political tact or expediency, followed the logic which led from military conscription to conscription of labour behind the lines; and he would have liked to make "labour battalions" a permanent part of the planned economy. But the end of the civil war and the coming of NEP relaxed all these efforts. In the Labour Code of 1922 compulsory labour is to be used only in "exceptional cases", defined as "struggle with elemental occurrences, lack of labour power for carrying out important state tasks", though penalties against "desertion from work" are still maintained. But NEP soon relegated the question of labour discipline to the background. Among the other blessings of capitalism it brought back unemployment, which imposes its own discipline on labour. Where there are too many men for too few jobs the problem of labour compulsion and direction does not arise.

Only when the first Five-Year Plan took up the slack of unemployment, when increased production became the all-important need, and there were once more too few men for too many jobs, did questions of labour discipline once more become acute. The way in which the Soviet Union tackled them is instructive for countries which, having committed themselves to policies of full employment, will be faced with similar problems. The methods adopted were eclectic and indicate no dogmatic or exclusive theory of labour discipline or labour incentives. There was no formal return to the labour conscription of the period of "war communism": the only "forced labour" in the Soviet Union of the 1930's was that of political and other prisoners who, collected together in great camps, were employed under conditions of captivity on public works. Nevertheless if formal compulsion was not applied to enforce the constitutional obligation to work, it was probably because less direct methods proved sufficient. In 1931, unemployment insurance was abolished on the ground that unemployment had ceased to exist; the institution of work-books operated as a further check; and severe penalties were imposed on "labour desertion", absenteeism and bad time-keeping, though the reiteration of decrees against these practices suggest that this legislation was no more effective than similar legislation in war-time Britain. Exactly how workers were recruited and how enterprises were prevented from competing against one another for scarce labour—a problem which was experienced in war-time Britain and will always recur in conditions of full employment under planning—is difficult to ascertain. It may be surmised that the organization of the trade unions was adequate for the purpose. When Sir Ernest Simon investigated the Moscow municipality in the 'thirties, he received this account of the recruitment of building operatives:

A certain rural area is allotted to the Moscow Building Trust; they send their agents out to this area and by agreement with the collective farms bring in seasonal workers. They work at the farm when they are needed, especially in sowing time and harvest, and put in the rest of the year building in Moscow.[1]

[1] E. D. Simon and others, *Moscow in the Making*, pp. 131–2.

Clearly such a system implies a substantial amount of "direction of labour" and probably also the provision by the trust of housing for its workers. There is perhaps not much direct guidance here for the western world. But a good many problems are foreshadowed which will confront all countries pursuing full employment policies.

The positive labour incentives adopted in the Soviet Union have been extraordinarily varied. The Soviet authorities have tried at one time or another most of the monetary incentives known to the capitalist system. Piece-rates have become the rule rather than the exception: the delegation of the Iron and Steel Trades Confederation to the Soviet Union in 1945 reported that all but 5% of the workers in heavy industry were on piece-rates, though the proportion was probably not so high before the war. There has been a progressive tendency to step up wage differentials for the benefit of the more efficient and more rapid worker. Fines for bad time-keeping have been matched by bonuses and prizes for high output. Stakhanovism, apart from its propaganda aspects, meant enormously increased monetary rewards for the exceptionally efficient. The delegates of the Iron and Steel Trades Confederation visited a strip mill which, by producing the highest output for the year in the Soviet Union, had won not only a banner but a bonus of a week's wages for its workers. What is perhaps more likely to find imitators in the west is the spread of economic incentives of a non-financial kind. The economic attraction of a job in the Soviet Union has for a long time past been measured not solely, and perhaps not mainly, by the monetary rewards, but by the value of the canteen and other similar facilities offered by the factory, of possible privileges or priorities in the matter of housing, and of access to closed shops. Some of these symptoms are beginning to appear in western countries.

The largest advance has, however, been made by the Soviet Union in the development of non-economic incentives. The first issue to be faced here is that of nationalization; for Soviet influence has everywhere done much to stimulate the demand of the workers for the nationalization of industry. But the Soviet example contains a warning as well as an encouragement. The first concrete application in Soviet Russia of the idea of nationalization was to place factories under the control of the workers who worked in them. This proved a complete fiasco. Factories cannot be run by a committee of workers; and the Soviet Government was quickly compelled in the interest of efficiency to restore the principle not merely of management, but of one-man management. Joint committees of workers and management, such as have been popular in recent years both in the Soviet Union and in western countries, do valuable work in minor questions of organization, in handling personal grievances and in the large and important field known as "welfare", but are not, and never can be, responsible for major decisions of policy. If nationalization has provided a stimulus to output in the Soviet Union, this has been due not so much to any additional control obtained by the worker over the concern in which he is employed as to the sense that all the means of production are now vested not in private employers, but in the workers' state which corporately represents the worker and stands primarily for his interests. This Soviet experience is probably valid for the western countries. There is no sufficient evidence that the attitude of the British miner or the British transport worker to his job will change because the particular enterprise in which he is employed is nationalized. But it might be radically changed by the realization that governmental power as a whole, including the control of industry, was vested in an authority representing his class and his interests.

Apart from the transfer of the means of production to public ownership, the Soviet Government has relied on many other non-economic incentives to increase the productivity of labour. At the outset of the revolution, Lenin believed that the publication of adequate statistics would explain to the worker "how much work and what kind of work must be done" [1] and that this knowledge would suffice to make him do it. While this expectation may seem rather too simple, the British authorities discovered during the war the high value, as an aid to productivity, of propaganda designed to explain to the worker the precise significance and purpose of the work on which he was engaged. Soviet theory and Soviet practice have steadily discouraged the attitude to work as merely something disagreeable undertaken perforce in order to gain the means of subsistence. This attitude is, in the Soviet view, appropriate to capitalism: under socialism work is something honourable, even pleasurable—a contribution by the worker to building up a society of which he is a full member. An attempt is made to render industrial work attractive, both by playing up the romance of the machine and by treating it as the symbol of the "advanced" culture towards which "backward" Russia is striving. Emulation is invoked as an incentive, both by the honour paid to individual "Stakhanovite" workers and by "socialist competition" between rival factories or groups. All this provokes serious reflexion in western countries, which will be required in conditions of full employment to develop fresh incentives for labour; and some of these methods have already been followed there during the war.

⋅ ⋅ ⋅ ⋅ ⋅

The attitude of the Soviet Union towards labour and towards social questions generally cannot be discussed without

[1] Lenin, *The Next Tasks of Soviet Power* (1918).

54

reference to the trade unions. Trade unions, which' grew up under capitalism to meet specifically capitalist conditions, were clearly destined to evolve with the evolution of capitalism, and to undergo a radical transformation when capitalism was succeeded by socialism. Hence the experience of the Soviet Union is likely to be highly significant for the western countries, even though it will not be exactly repeated or slavishly imitated there.

Marx praised the trade unions as "a rampart for the workers in their struggle with the capitalists",[1] but had nothing to say of their place under socialism. In general, Marxists before 1917 tended to ignore or play down the future role of trade unions, while syndicalists treated them as the main elements in the economic, or even the political, structure of the future order. This fundamental division emerged immediately after the Bolshevik revolution. Nationalization of industry began in the form of the taking over of enterprises by workers' committees. But this decentralized and potentially syndicalist conception of the control of industry soon clashed with the demand for centralized control of the whole national economy by the state, i.e. planning. In this collision, the trade unions, or at any rate their headquarters organizations, tended to side with the state against unruly local leaders—a situation which has since often reproduced itself elsewhere. Centralization won all along the line, partly owing to the inefficiency and inadequacy of locally organized workers' control of industry, partly owing to the impetus given to central planning by the onset of civil war.

The relation between state and trade unions remained, however, unsolved; and this became the subject of a controversy which was at its height in 1920–21 and was not finally allayed till the expulsion of Trotsky in 1927. At one

[1] Marx, *The Poverty of Philosophy* (English trans.), p. 187.

extreme Trotsky stood for the view that the trade unions had no independent functions to perform under socialism, and should be taken over lock, stock and barrel by the state; at the other extreme Tomsky stood for the completest possible independence of the trade unions. The compromise supported by Lenin made the best of both worlds. Lenin believed that the trade unions, being closer to the masses and less tainted by bureaucracy than the official organs of government, could serve both as a valuable link between government and people and as a good recruiting-ground for public officials. The independence of the trade unions was affirmed against the Trotskyists who wished to turn them into departments of the state. On the other hand, the trade unions could not be wholly independent in matters of policy; for were not both government and unions subject to the general directives of the party? The first Congress of the Red Trade Union International (*Profintern*) declared in a resolution that "the idea of the independence of the trade union movement must be energetically and emphatically rejected".

The compromise of 1921 tightened rather than relaxed the bonds between the unions and the state. The constitution of the All-Russian Congress of Trade Unions adopted in 1922 laid it down that the Congress should "draft all legislation for the defence of the economic and cultural interests of trade unionists and take measures to have these bills passed by the competent government departments". Already in 1920 Milyutin had described the People's Commissariat for Labour as "almost completely fused with the trade unions both in its work and in the composition of its chief directors".[1] The principle was now established that the People's Commissar for Labour should be appointed on the nomination of the All-Russian Congress of Trade Unions; those who remember

[1] V. P. Milyutin, *Istoriya Ekonomicheskogo Razvitiya SSSR*, p. 169.

that a British coalition Government in 1940 appointed as Minister of Labour a prominent trade union leader who had hitherto played no part in political life and was not even a member of Parliament, and that a Labour Government appointed to the same office in 1945 the president of the Trade Union Congress, may conclude that the Soviet usage has found *de facto* application elsewhere. In 1933 the Commissariat of Labour was abolished and its functions handed over to the organs of the All-Union Congress of Trade Unions. In ordinary life it is a matter of some importance whether the tiger eats the man or the man the tiger; where the parties to the transaction are political institutions, the difference is less clearly marked. Some people may have reflected in 1933 that, if Trotsky in 1920 had reversed his proposal, the logical result at which he aimed might have been achieved with less friction and with less delay. The twin functions of controlling labour and promoting the interests of labour become so closely intertwined that they ultimately merge.

These issues of the relation of trade unions to the state reflect far-reaching developments in trade unionism which are beginning to make themselves felt in other countries besides the Soviet Union. Under capitalism trade unions were concerned to secure the enjoyment by the worker—whether in the form of higher wages, shorter hours or improved material conditions—of as large a proportion as possible of the product of his labour. Under socialism the worker *ex hypothesi* receives the whole product of his labour, less appropriate deductions for amortization and for various social or public services. In these conditions trade unions which defend the worker's interest will no longer need to concern themselves in the distribution of the product; the interest of the worker is now to increase the size of the product. Hence the chief task of the trade unions under socialism is to increase the produc-

57

tivity of labour. "The *organization of production* is the chief task of the trade unions in the epoch of the proletarian dictatorship", wrote Bukharin and Preobrazhensky in their famous *ABC of Communism* published in 1919 and translated into many languages;[1] and the first All-Russian Congress of Trade Unions explicitly decreed:

> The centre of gravity of the work of the trade unions at the present moment must be transferred to the sphere of economic organization. The trade unions, being class organizations of the proletariat built up on the productive principle, must take on themselves the chief work for organizing production and restoring the shattered productive forces of the country.

The Soviet trade unions throughout their history have regarded the stimulation of production as one of their principal functions. Nor is this simply because the history of the Soviet Union has been a record of almost continuous national emergency: it results from the logical position of trade unions under socialism.

The same logic applies to admissibility of strikes under socialism. Under capitalism the strike is an expression of class conflict: it is used as an economic weapon against private employers or as a political weapon against the ruling class. Under socialism there are no private employers and the workers constitute the ruling class, so that strikes become meaningless. It is true that the trade unions represent certain interests of the workers and that their interests may clash with others, even in a socialist economy. (There is, for example, always the question how much of the product of labour should be allocated to wages or other amenities of immediate advantage to the workers and how much to investment in long-term projects.) But such clashes of interest, which are devoid of

[1] Bukharin and Preobrazhensky, *ABC of Communism*, ch. XII, p. 98.

any class basis, occur in a capitalist economy, e.g. between industrialists and farmers; and no one supposes that these would be settled by a strike. Just as in Great Britain a dispute between, say, the Board of Trade and Ministry of Agriculture would be settled by a Cabinet decision, so a dispute between the Soviet trade unions and some other Soviet organ would be settled not by a strike, but by a decision of the higher Soviet authorities—or conceivably of the party. Strikes have not been formally made illegal, but they have, in the official view, ceased to have any sense. They would certainly not be supported by the trade unions, and would probably be treated as a punishable offence, though whether the punishment would fall on the strikers or on the management against which they had struck might depend on the view taken by the higher authorities of the case. There does not appear to be any record of a strike in the Soviet Union for many years past.

Some hostile critics have been tempted to regard all this argument as make-believe and to suggest that what has really happened in the Soviet Union is that the trade unions have been put in their place by a totalitarian regime. But the curious thing is that marked symptoms of a similar development have appeared in the trade union movements of western Europe which, in spite of an anti-Soviet bias, have sometimes paid to the Soviet trade unions the sincerest form of flattery. The economic reason for this development is clear, and explains why it has not yet perceptibly spread to the United States or, perhaps, to other oversea countries. Under 19th century capitalism output was so constantly expanding that the trade unions had only to interest themselves in a fair division of the product of labour; the margin on which they could draw was so great that they were not called on to worry about the size of the product. But this kind of capitalism scarcely exists any longer outside the United States; and there too it is already threatened. For 20 years or more apprehensions caused by the threatened diminution in the size of the cake have produced a marked tendency for employers and trade unions to join hands in advocating restrictive measures directed against the foreigner or against the consumer. Today such measures are seen to be inadequate and perhaps in the long run suicidal. In the decaying capitalism of the mid-20th century, it has become clear that failure to raise output will be as detrimental to the workers as to the capitalists; and what is required by the interests of the workers is, paradoxical as it may appear to old-fashioned trade unionists, an alliance between workers and management to raise output. Even under capitalism such an alliance has become necessary. The report on *Post-War Reconstruction* approved by the Trades Union Congress in September 1944 cautiously admitted that the trade union movement was concerned, among other things, "with increasing the size of the real national income".[1] Under socialism, with industries nationalized, this attitude becomes logical as well as necessary. We may not be as far as we now appear from a pronouncement by the Trade Union Congress on the lines of the resolution of the first All-Russian Congress of Trade Unions nearly 30 years ago that the chief task of the trade unions is to "organize production and restore the shattered productive forces of the country".

Nor perhaps are the western countries as far removed as appears at first sight from the Soviet view of the obligation to work. When labour exchanges were instituted in Great Britain in 1909 to cope with unemployment, Sidney Webb wrote that one of the advantages of "the public organization of the labour market by means of labour exchanges" was that it "enables the state (as the socialists and trade unionists are at one with the rest of the world in demanding) to make it

[1] *Post-War Reconstruction: Interim Report* (T.U.C. 1944), p. 7.

more disagreeable for the 'work-shy' ".[1] It is the prospect of full employment, not merely as a by-product of war, but as a normal condition of peace, which has begun to transform the attitude of the trade union movement to this question. "In the circumstances in which the threat of the 'sack' no longer operates in industry," observes the above quoted report on *Post-War Reconstruction*, "a system of self-discipline which is approved by the workers and undertaken by their collective organization will be required".[2] A corollary of this development is the changed attitude to strikes. In Great Britain, at any rate, it is many years since an important strike was sponsored or supported by a responsible trade union. The reason is obvious. British trade unions, like Soviet trade unions, stand so well with the ruling authorities that they can achieve better results by negotiating with them than by fighting them. Hence the trade unions draw closer and closer to the organs of government and co-operate with authority to restrain their own unruly followers. It may not be as safe in Great Britain as it is in the Soviet Union to predict that there will be no more major strikes; but it is equally safe in both countries to predict that any such strikes would be conducted not by the trade unions but against the trade unions. In this respect the western world is travelling far more rapidly than most people yet realize along the Soviet path.

[1] *Cambridge Modern History*, XII, p. 765.
[2] *Post-War Reconstruction: Interim Report* (T.U.C. 1944), p. 23.

IV

THE IMPACT ON INTERNATIONAL
RELATIONS

THE diplomacy of the 19th century, i.e. the conduct of relations with other countries, was a highly specialized trade.
Such of its activities as were not purely formal or ceremonial
were political; its principal preoccupation was the balance of
power in the so-called "concert of Europe". It concerned
itself with economic matters only in so far as it promoted
commercial treaties to secure non-discrimination between
traders of different nations or intervened to prevent discrimination in practice against traders of its own nation; and it
did not concern itself with publicity at all. Today the conduct
of foreign affairs falls into three main sectors with many subsidiary ramifications—politics, economics and finance, and
publicity. No doubt this enlargement of the sphere of international relations has been a natural consequence of the enlargement of the sphere of the state; and, though it has for
the most part occurred since 1917, it would be absurd to
attribute it to the influence of what has happened in the
Soviet Union. Nevertheless it is there that the enlargement of
the functions of the state, with all that that entails, has been
carried to its furthest point; and analysis will show that the
Soviet impact on the conduct of international relations, espe-

cially but not exclusively in the spheres of economics and publicity, has been direct and important.

. . . . .

In international trade and finance, the dominant factor in the Soviet Union has been the foreign trade monopoly. It was established in 1918, survived without modification throughout the NEP period, and has been one of the most stable and, so far as the evidence goes, successful of all Soviet institutions. The present Commissar for Foreign Trade, Mikoyan, has held office continuously since the 1920's, and is generally regarded as one of the most influential of leading Soviet officials. The Commissariat conducts the whole foreign trade of the Soviet Union, the Soviet trading agencies abroad being directly responsible to it. This system presents certain obvious advantages; and it is interesting to observe how other countries have sought to reap these advantages by indirect devices without committing themselves to the full implications of a monopoly of foreign trade.

The monopoly of foreign trade, by eliminating individual traders and by making the state the principal in all commercial transactions, wipes out the distinction between commercial treaties and commercial contracts. It places the organization and resources of the state behind every trading transaction. In a world where every country had a state monopoly of foreign trade, every commercial contract would be an agreement between states. In a world where only one country has such a monopoly, that country enjoys certain tangible advantages over its competitors. The most obvious of them is that it presents a united front to the world while playing off ⟨ traders of other countries against one another. But there are other more important advantages, some of which have been referred to in a previous chapter. The monopoly of foreign trade makes it possible to take effective account of the real interdependence of imports and exports, since the same authority controls both, whereas the interests of the private importer and the private exporter are separate and, at any rate in the short run, no kind of conformity need be established between them. The monopoly of foreign trade enables the country possessing it both to safeguard vital national industries and to foster "infant industries" without resort to the clumsy device of the tariff. It makes possible a national calculation of costs both of exports and of imports to the economy as a whole, which may differ widely from a calculation of profit and loss made by the particular firm which handles them. In brief, it facilitates a comprehensive planning of foreign trade, not merely at the moment, but perhaps for some years ahead, in terms likely to prove most advantageous to the national economy. A subsidiary advantage is that it enables national economic policy to be brought into line with other aspects of the nation's foreign policy.

Under the economic stress of the early 1930's the western world became dimly conscious of these advantages, and attempts were made to achieve the same results by a series of roundabout devices—barter agreements, under which state A undertakes to purchase so much meat from state B in return for the purchase of a corresponding value of coal by state B from state A; quota agreements, by which state A agrees to take certain proportions of its requirements of a given commodity from states B, C and D; and clearing and payment agreements under which the parties agree that all payments for imports and exports shall be made through a central fund, so that the state, while not intervening in particular commercial transactions, is able to control the sum total of them. But these half-hearted devices had two specific drawbacks. In the management of foreign trade, as in internal planning, the Soviet Union had begun by controlling particular commodities and moved on to global control. In the western world, the devices in question gave governments a certain amount of global control, but deprived them of the possibility of controlling particular transactions, and thereby hampered their efficiency. Secondly, these devices had the adventitious practical drawback of running counter to the canons of *laissez-faire* orthodoxy in international trade in a way in which, paradoxically enough, the monopoly of foreign trade did not. All these devices could reasonably be held to involve formal discrimination by the state between transactions with different foreign countries. Where, as under the monopoly of foreign trade, the state is direct buyer and seller, the charge of discrimination cannot arise; for nobody has ever disputed the right of buyer or seller to select his market at his own discretion. For this reason the Soviet Union has always been able to sign commercial agreements providing for non-discrimination without the slightest embarrassment. It has been said with some plausibility that the only condition on which Great Britain could honour the obligations resulting from the Bretton Woods agreement would be the establishment of a British monopoly of foreign trade.

The monopoly of foreign trade had important repercussions on international finance. It enabled the Soviet Union to divorce domestic price policy from considerations of world prices, or, in other words, to sever all connexion between the domestic and the international value of its currency. It was some time before the Soviet authorities themselves learned this lesson. In 1924, following western precept and example, they stabilized their currency in terms of gold on the lines of strictest financial orthodoxy, establishing a new monetary unit, the chervonetz, for the purpose. But it soon appeared that the stability of the chervonetz could not be maintained without applying at home the deflationary policies of orthodox capitalism; and this, even under NEP, would have been more than the regime could bear. In 1926 the import and export of the chervonetz were prohibited; and while the external value of the chervonetz was maintained at a conventional level for use in foreign transactions, this no longer had any relation to the purchasing power of the chervonetz as determined by the price level at home. This practice was imitated by Germany and by several other European countries in the 1930's. Today it is almost universal. Rates of exchange between national currencies are now everywhere the result not of the unimpeded operations of supply and demand or of respective price levels in the countries concerned, but of decisions of national policy; and everywhere the tendency has been to establish sufficient control over foreign trade to enable a policy of price-fixing to be maintained at home without interference from an uncontrolled influx of supplies from abroad.

It may be well, however, to enter a caveat against the idea that all the successful practices which became current in international trade in the 1930's were derived from Soviet example. On the contrary, although the Soviet Union was the inventor of the monopoly of foreign trade which made these practices possible, it was not itself economically strong enough to exploit its advantage in the way in which this was subsequently done by other countries, notably Germany. An instance of this was the failure of the Soviet Union, in spite of its trade monopoly, to insulate itself against the consequences of the world slump of 1930–33. A country can protect itself from trade depression elsewhere provided it has means to organize its trade as a national unit, and provided also that it is a large enough importer to obtain favourable terms from those who sell to it and a large enough exporter to secure favourable terms from those who need to buy from

66

it, and so maintain both the volume and the value of its trade. This was one of the ways in which Great Britain, even without direct state trading, achieved a rapid recovery after 1932 through the instrumentality of quota, clearing and payments agreements. The Soviet Union, even with the full monopoly of foreign trade, was not a large enough trader to influence conditions and prices on the world market, and what are called the terms of trade turned against it: in other words it had to pay for reduced imports with larger quantities of exports.

The same economic weakness of the Soviet Union prevented it from being a pioneer in international economic planning, this being not only a logical step from planning for the nation to planning for some larger unit, but also a step which could have found full support in Soviet ideology. Within the Soviet Union planning was one of the most powerful instruments for cutting across national divisions and welding the diverse national republics and territories into a single economic unit possessing a common loyalty and common political consciousness. But in spite of some utopian dreams nourished in the early days of the revolution, the foreign trade of the Soviet Union was never sufficiently developed, and never occupied a sufficiently large part in the economy of any foreign country, to permit of any international policy of common economic action and planning under Soviet leadership. It was German economic strength which enabled Germany in the later 1930's to dominate the markets of eastern and south-eastern Europe, mainly by the simple method of providing the one available large-scale market for the products of these countries. It was German economic strength, combined with German military strength, which enabled Germany to effect, in the abnormal conditions of war, that forced integration of the European economy known as the "new order". Beyond doubt the Soviet authorities have studied these lessons and hope to be able in future to exploit their monopoly of foreign trade more fully, at any rate in central and eastern Europe. This hope is apparent in the Soviet commercial agreements with Roumania and Hungary of 1945, which provide for bulk exchange of products between these countries and the Soviet Union.

If this hope is realized, other countries will be compelled to set up forms of state trading in order to be able to compete with the Soviet foreign trade monopoly. In 1940 Great Britain set up a state trading company, the United Kingdom Commercial Corporation, to push British trade in the Balkan countries against all-pervading German competition. The German invasion of the Balkans temporarily drove it from that field. But during the war the U.K.C.C. conducted trading operations throughout the Middle East, with the Soviet Union and in many other parts of the world where private traders could have made no headway; and it created several subsidiary corporations in foreign countries on much the same footing as the Soviet trade organizations abroad. How far its function will continue in time of peace is still unsettled. But the policy of organized trade for which it stands cannot safely be abandoned. Great Britain already has bulk purchase agreements for specific commodities with some of the Dominions, and during the war made similar agreements with other countries for war purposes. To take one instance, she will be obliged to conclude bulk purchase contracts for Greek products if Greece is to be kept within the British sphere of influence: the omission of any such arrangement was one of the weaknesses of the Anglo-Greek economic and financial agreement of January, 1946. So long as economic action remains a major part of foreign policy—and there is nothing to suggest any diminution of this tendency—the monopoly of foreign trade provides the Soviet Union with the most effective possible instrument for conducting such action; and other countries will be driven more and more insistently to set up similar institutions.

.　　　　.　　　　.　　　　.

The impact of the Soviet Union on international relations in the sphere of economic policy has been less conspicuous than in the sphere of propaganda—or publicity as it is more politely called by those who speak of their own efforts. No doubt propaganda in the broad sense of the term is not new. Bismarck distorted the Ems telegram in order to exacerbate French feeling; the French revolutionaries, and later Napoleon, appealed for sympathy to the rising middle classes throughout Europe and incited them to rebel against their rulers; an American scholar as recently as 1940 published a work on *Propaganda in Germany in the Thirty Years' War;* and even Philip of Macedon is said to have had fifth columns in the city states of ancient Greece. But propaganda in the contemporary sense of a process organized and carried out by officials appointed for the purpose as part of the normal conduct of foreign policy is a quite recent phenomenon, which owes much to Soviet inspiration and example.

Like other modern developments in which the Soviet Union has played a leading part, the organized use of propaganda in international relations was a product of the first world war. It was then discovered that propaganda directed to enemy soldiers and civilians might help to sap their morale and hasten the enemy's defeat. In the later stages of the war, Great Britain used it against Germany and, more effectively, against Austria-Hungary; Germany used it when she sent Lenin and his fellow Bolsheviks into Russia in the sealed train; the Soviet leaders used it at Brest-Litovsk and elsewhere in an attempt to disintegrate the German armies operating against them.

69

What the Soviet leaders did was not to invent a new technique, but to systematize and develop it and to realize its potentialities as an instrument of foreign policy in time of peace. If they did not always attain the objective of winning support for Soviet policy, this was certainly not due to any imperfections in their use of the instrument. It was rather because they were successful enough to inspire in the minds of foreign governments so much fear of "Bolshevik propaganda" that those governments were deterred from collaborating whole-heartedly with the Soviet Union even when their national interest might have seemed to dictate that course.

Historically it was the weakness of the Soviet Government in other forms of power which impelled them in the early days of the regime to develop the new weapon with so much vigour. But the development was none the less logical. The industrial revolution, which provided the technical facilities for large-scale propaganda, notably the popular press, the film and the radio, also created the conditions which made its use necessary. The importance of propaganda is a symptom and product of the new mass civilization. All government rests in some degree on the capacity of the ruler or rulers to persuade some body of opinion—if only the opinion of a pretorian guard—that their rule is desirable. But it is only in recent times, and more specifically since the industrial revolution, that the masses of the workers have been included among those whom it was necessary or useful to persuade; and it is only in recent times that science and invention have placed at the disposal of the state the material instruments necessary for the persuasion of large masses of people. It was therefore appropriate not only that the development of propaganda as an instrument of policy should have marked the culmination of the industrial revolution, but that it should have been carried to its highest point by the country which has realized most fully the potentialities of mass civilization. The primacy of the Soviet Union in the use of propaganda in international affairs is largely due to the frank appeal which it makes to the masses. The propaganda of other countries still tends to be too intellectual in character, and to direct its appeal too exclusively to a select class, to have the same far-reaching effects as Soviet propaganda.

Soviet propaganda enjoys the further advantage of emanating from a powerful political unit which claims to be the repository of universal truth and the missionary of a universal gospel. This was the spirit of the first Soviet broadcast messages which were addressed "To All", and purported to be equally concerned with the welfare of the workers of every country. In March 1919 Lenin created—in the shape of the Communist International—a propaganda organization to spread the gospel throughout the world. Alone among the principal governments of the world, the Soviet Government never possessed a department of its own for international propaganda. The universal appeal of Soviet propaganda clearly gave it an enormous advantage over the propaganda of countries which sought in the main to advertise their own national qualities and achievements. The international membership of the Communist International made it a more effective instrument than the national propaganda organizations of other countries in as much as Soviet propaganda was partly or mainly conducted by citizens of the countries to which it was directed; and this advantage was not lost with the dissolution of the International in 1943 since its work was carried on in the same spirit by national communist parties. In spite of the volume of international propaganda to which the Soviet example has given rise, no other nation has been able to emulate this characteristic of Soviet propaganda on any considerable scale. The international appeal of western democracy petered

71

out after 1919. The international appeal of fascism never got much beyond a negative attempt to counter communism: its characteristic achievement was the futile "anti-Comintern pact". The international appeal of communism was in the early years one of the main instruments of Soviet foreign policy and, in general, of the Soviet impact on the western world. Beyond doubt this appeal was subsequently compromised by realization of the extent to which international communism has in fact adapted itself to the day-to-day needs of Soviet foreign policy. But the Soviet Union has a long start in this field. No other country has yet been nearly so successful in making international propaganda an integral part of its machinery for the conduct of foreign policy.

The essence of propaganda as an instrument of foreign policy is an appeal to potentially influential groups in another country in the hope that they will influence the policy of their own government. This aim was crudely apparent in such manifestations of propaganda as Woodrow Wilson's appeal to the Italian people in April 1919 to disown the annexationist policy pursued by the Italian delegation in Paris, or in Soviet appeals to workers of other countries to resist action unfavourable to the Soviet Union. If the United States spends money on propaganda in Great Britain, the purpose is to make British opinion pro-American and therefore likely to induce the government to pursue policies acceptable to the United States; if Great Britain conducts propaganda in France, the object is the same. International propaganda is in this sense always an interference in another country's affairs; it seeks, through exercising political influence on its recipients, to mould the policy and limit the freedom of action of the government of the receiving country. But here we come to an important discrepancy, due to constitutional differences, between the Soviet Union and the western world. The Soviet Government, taking the realistic view of propaganda as a weapon which should be used by oneself, but the use of which should if possible be denied to others, makes every effort to discourage foreign propaganda and to exclude it from the Soviet Union; and the thoroughness of its administrative control, together with the limited number of individual radio sets available, makes this task relatively easy. The Soviet Union is therefore ahead of the rest of the world both in the conduct of its own propaganda and in its capacity to nullify the propaganda of other countries. It should, however, be noted that this latter advantage is enjoyed partly in virtue of the material backwardness of Soviet civilization and of the isolation of the Soviet Union from the rest of the world. Nazi Germany, before and during the war, endeavoured to follow the Soviet example, but was far less successful than the Soviet Union in excluding foreign propaganda.

The western democracies have been placed in a somewhat embarrassing position by the development of propaganda as an instrument of foreign policy. Freedom of opinion is a tenet of the democratic creed; and democratic governments are inhibited, both for practical and for ideological reasons, from seeking to prevent the dissemination of opinion even when promoted by a foreign agency. Nevertheless the western countries, under the impact of Soviet example, have already admitted some reservations to this principle. In 1921 Great Britain concluded with Soviet Russia the first international agreement in which an attempt was made to restrict propaganda. In succeeding years such agreements were not uncommon. One of the latest of them was an agreement of 1938 between the British and Italian Governments renouncing "any attempt by either of them to employ the methods of publicity and propaganda at its disposal in order to injure the interests of the other". Such agreements were obviously not susceptible of precise application, and were never effective. Totalitarian countries, even without them, were on the whole in a position to protect themselves against foreign propaganda; democratic countries, even where they had weakened their own principles by entering into such agreements at all, were incapable of enforcing them.

A method employed by the British Government with far greater success—and imitated by many other governments—was the institution of a press department at the Foreign Office which issues regular information and guidance on the British point of view to the British press and to such parts of the foreign press as are amenable to it. Its services to the foreign press may be regarded as part of British propaganda to foreign countries. Its services to the home press are more significant and less familiar. It easily makes itself indispensable, since the Foreign Office has at its disposal a large volume of interesting and important news not accessible in any other way. Its function of selection gives it an enormous power to mould opinion. The mere decision to release or withhold certain information, or certain types of information, about Ruritania may profoundly affect public emotions about that country and radically change the public attitude towards it; and the discreet advice which the department sometimes gives to play up or to play down points of friction with particular countries is scarcely needed. The same carefully selected information, and the same guidances and advice, reach the B.B.C. through different channels, and are still more effective, since the B.B.C. lacks even that tradition of independence which still clings to some organs of the press. Thus the British Government has created an exceedingly adroit and subtle instrument which serves not only to promote positive propaganda but to counter foreign propaganda, both by directly refuting it, and by discrediting the sources from which it comes. This development, like other developments of propaganda as an instrument of foreign policy, has implications which are perhaps not wholly reassuring for democracy; for it indicates how easily governments can mould opinion on a subject on which the private citizen can have little experience and few alternative sources of information. But, owing partly to the growth of mass civilization, and partly to the stimulus of Soviet example, propaganda has come to stay as an instrument of foreign policy; and a nation which organizes opinion, like the country which organizes its trade and finance, will inevitably be at an advantage over a nation which still adheres to the self-denying ordinances of *laissez-faire*.

It is sometimes argued that it is meaningless to discuss the technique of propaganda without discussing the validity of the ideas which the propagandist is attempting to convey. This does not seem to be wholly true. It would be useless to have a perfect system of export and import controls and an enlightened currency policy, if the economic resources of the country were too slender to sustain them: yet discussion of the relative merits of different economic policies is not meaningless. Nevertheless it should be frankly admitted that the success of propaganda probably depends in the long run less on the technical skill with which it is conducted than on the appeal of the ideas behind it to those to whom it is directed. Few people nowadays agree with the simple explanation of Pope Pius XI, who in his Encyclical of 1937 *Divini Redemptoris* attributed the success of communism to "a propaganda so truly diabolical that the world has perhaps never witnessed its like before". It has already been suggested that the success of Soviet propaganda has been largely due both to its appeal to the masses and to its international character. If western civilization fails to develop ideas which appear equally valid in these respects, the advantage will continue to be on the

75

side of the Soviet propagandists. The interplay of military and economic power is thus complicated by a battle of ideologies, waged partly though not exclusively on a basis of class, and now being fought out in the Balkans, in the Middle East and elsewhere. If it requires more precise definition, it can perhaps be defined in terms of the struggle between western and Soviet conceptions of democracy discussed in a previous chapter. Clearly this issue, as well as issues of power, was involved in the diplomatic clashes of the first months of 1946 between the western Powers and the Soviet Union.

. . . . .

The influence of the Soviet Union on international relations has been most apparent in the new importance now everywhere attached to international economics and international propaganda. Its influence on traditional political and diplomatic relations has been less tangible and less easily defined, but not for this reason negligible. The initial impression is somewhat paradoxical. In the first months of the revolution there was much talk of the impact of Soviet methods on the old diplomacy. Secrecy was denounced; the secret treaties of the Tsarist regime were published in a blaze of righteous indignation; and proclamations by radio largely replaced diplomatic notes as the chosen Soviet method of addressing other countries. But these practices did not survive the first flush of revolutionary enthusiasm. They were dictated partly by the anomalous position in which the Soviet Government found itself, boycotted by the capitalist world and unrecognized by any foreign government, partly by the weakness resulting from this position which made its international revolutionary appeal one of the few assets of the regime. As the Soviet Government became internationally established and recognized, concluded commercial and political treaties with capitalist governments and swung over from world revolution to the pursuit of "socialism in one country", more orthodox methods of conducting foreign policy were quickly restored. This did not mean that the Soviet Government abandoned its use of economic controls and of propaganda as instruments of foreign policy. But in the conduct of ordinary diplomatic relations the ultimate effect of the Soviet impact on international affairs was not to call for a new diplomacy, but to sound the retreat towards something older still.

How this came about can be easily seen. What passed for the new diplomacy in the formative years of Soviet policy was Woodrow Wilson's application to international affairs of the basic doctrines and assumptions of 19th century liberal democracy, of belief in the natural harmony of interest between nations, in the impartiality and the efficacy of enlightened and independent public opinion, and in the settlement of disputes by appeal to reason in public debate; and this ideology, of which the League of Nations was the chief exemplar and exponent, was freely invoked to discredit the Soviet Union. The Soviet leaders therefore had a double reason for disliking and distrusting the new Wilsonian diplomacy. In the first place, it sprang from *bourgeois* liberalism, which had always been anathema to Marxists and regarded by them as a cloak for material class interests; and, secondly, the use to which the new diplomacy was put by the capitalist Powers seemed all too surely to confirm Marx's diagnosis. Not unnaturally the directors of Soviet policy reacted strongly against it, turning away not so much to class warfare, which was now recognized as an inadequate guide to the conduct of foreign relations, but to older conceptions of interest and power which were less familiar, or at any rate, less openly avowed, in the 20th century than they had been in the two preceding centuries. In other words, while the Soviet Government continued to indulge on occasion for propaganda purposes in

idealistic gestures such as Mr. Litvinov's plan for total disarmament, Soviet foreign policy in general tended to be
couched in more "realistic" terms than those of other Powers
and thus to promote a reaction towards "realism".

The view that "ideals" are a cloak for "interests" is Marxist,
though by no means exclusively Marxist. In some measure it
is obviously well founded, and nowhere has it probably been
truer than in the conduct of international relations. Even in
the 19th century Walewski, the French Foreign Minister,
had remarked to Bismarck that it was the business of the
diplomat to cloak the interests of his country in the language
of universal justice. But in an epoch when statesmen had no
cause to fear that their confidential diplomatic conversations
would be reported in the press on the following day, or that
the text of their diplomatic notes would appear in print in a
matter of weeks or months, international affairs were conducted in an atmosphere of greater frankness and realism.
Those responsible for conducting them were not in essence
more honest or more sincere than their successors today—
perhaps indeed less so; but they saw less reason to disguise in
elegant circumlocutions their primary preoccupation with
national interest. After 1918 the growth of popular concern
in international affairs, the Wilsonian ideology of enlightened
public opinion, and the establishment of the League of Nations made it seem more important than ever, especially in
the western democracies, to bring foreign policy into line
with the proclaimed ideals and even with the formal rules of
the Covenant; and this sometimes entailed a larger measure of
window-dressing or sheer hypocrisy than had been customary
in the franker days of 19th century diplomacy. The historian
of the future will learn far less of the unvarnished truth from
the diplomatic documents of the past twenty-five years than
from those of any previous period; the League of Nations in

particular made fashionable a set of elaborate formulas which ingeniously concealed from the unwary the real motives of the negotiators. Whatever the other merits or demerits of the conduct of international affairs between the two wars, there was more humbug about it than probably in any previous period of recorded history.

This state of affairs lent itself readily to Soviet "debunking", which was the more inevitable since the Soviet Union was at this time an unprivileged Power excluded from the favours of international society. The Soviet propagandists of the 1920's could hardly be blamed if they pointed out that British policy in Egypt or United States policy in Nicaragua was more concerned with British or American interests respectively than with self-determination or the rights of small nations. No doubt, as the Soviet Union resumed the status of a Great Power, it developed an equally ingenuous casuistry of its own, such as was required to justify the Soviet-German pact of August 1939 while continuing to damn the Munich agreement of September 1938. But Soviet casuistry seemed less important than its democratic counterpart, partly because it convinced fewer people, partly because the men who actually conducted foreign policy were themselves less infected by it. Soviet negotiators frequently shock the western world by the frankness with which they state their demands. This does not necessarily mean that these demands are more exorbitant than those of other Great Powers in the past, or perhaps even in the present, but that less trouble is taken to veil them in the decent garments which modern diplomatic fashions require. There is no doubt that it would be far easier to negotiate with the Soviet Union in terms of conflicting national interests than in terms of ideals in the sincerity of which the Soviet negotiators, at any rate, have no belief, and that Soviet influence is leading back to a franker avowal of national interests as the motive force in international relations than was fashionable in the discreeter Wilsonian epoch.

A greater propensity to question the sincerity of professed ideals is accompanied by a keener insistence on the role of power in the conduct of foreign policy. The doubtless apocryphal quip attributed to Stalin "Who is the Pope? How many divisions has he?" neatly expresses Soviet appreciation of the element of power inherent in every international relation or transaction. In the period between the wars some such corrective was certainly required to the current illusion that "power politics" had been, or could be, conjured out of existence by the wave of a Genevese wand. It was sincerely believed at this time in many quarters that public debate was an effective way of settling international disputes without recourse to the influence of power and, indeed, without regard to the rival strength of the parties to the dispute. This notion was consistently contested by Soviet spokesmen; and, after the Soviet Union joined the League of Nations, its main efforts at Geneva were directed to putting "teeth" into the Covenant. Even today, however, western democratic leaders, misled by the misunderstood analogy of their own institutions, are far too apt to regard vigour and eloquence in public debate as constituting in themselves influential factors in the conduct of international relations. When Palmerston banged the despatch box with his fist and made provocative speeches, the effect was due not to the weight of the fist or the strength of the language, but to the overwhelming preponderance of the British navy and to the willingness of the British Government to use it. Today the idea apparently still prevails that to bang the despatch box with a fist twice as weighty as Palmerston's and to use language twice as strong will compensate for the lack of British preponderance in ships and air squadrons and military divisions. This view is both seductive and dangerous; it encourages the comfortable belief, which played so much havoc in British foreign policy between the wars, that words can be a substitute for deeds. One healthy effect of the assumption of an active role by the Soviet Union in international affairs is an increasing realization of the importance of the power factor.

A corollary of the emphasis on power is an emphasis on the difference between great and small nations. Soviet theory has always pointed to the unreality, even in domestic politics, of "one man, one vote", so long as this formal equality is nullified by a real inequality of social and economic status. This unreality is a thousand times more conspicuous in a system based on a formal equality of nations, or on the principle "one nation, one vote". The issue at stake is not equality before the law, but equality in the determination of those questions of conflicting interests and rivalries for power which, in international as in domestic affairs, are a matter for political, not legal, decision. Soviet influence has consistently supported the view that there can be no political equality between great and small Powers, and that a system based on the pretence of an equality which does not exist is necessarily a sham. This does not, of course, mean that there are two hard and fast categories of great and small, or that there are any rigid lines of demarcation at all, but that in all international issues of a political character power acts as a differentiating factor, and must be recognized as such.

Such differentiation profoundly affects every problem of international organization. Until thirty years ago the distinction between great and small Powers was an unchallenged assumption of international politics, the constant rule and practice being that only Great Powers took part in major international conferences and major political decisions. The 19th century concert of Europe was the perfected form of this assumption. As recently as 1918 such early stalwarts of the League of Nations as Lord Cecil and Colonel House took it for granted that membership of the Council of the League, its executive organ, would be confined to the Great Powers; and Lord Cecil gave the cogent reason for this view that "the smaller Powers would in any case not exercise any considerable influence".[1] The Soviet negotiators at the Dumbarton Oaks and San Francisco conferences consistently sought to reserve the prerogative of major international decisions to the Great Powers, and resisted, though not always successfully, every concession designed to give the smaller nations an effective voice in political issues. The famous veto of the Great Powers on decisions of the Security Council is almost the last stronghold in the Charter of the United Nations of the predominant position of the Great Powers. In the same spirit the Soviet Government long struggled to maintain the exclusiveness of the "Big Three", since these are the only nations with sufficient resources to make their power effective in any part of the world. To admit China and France to participate in the discussion of the affairs of regions (say, the Balkans) where neither has any potential power at all was, on the Soviet view, irrelevant and illogical.

The aim of recent Soviet policy in the field of international organization has thus been in effect to return as far as possible to the principles of the concert of Europe, now extended to cover the world. The return to the past is, however, in part fallacious. The smaller nations can no longer remain, as they remained in the 19th century, neutral and remote from the decisive currents of international affairs. Sooner or later they will be drawn into the orbit of one or other of the Great Powers, so that the prospect which apparently confronts us is that of two, three or more constellations of power,

[1] Miller, *The Drafting of the Covenant*, II, p. 61.

each of them having one Great Power as its nucleus. This is clearly the trend not only of Soviet policy throughout eastern Europe and northern Asia, but also of American policy which is seeking a consolidation of power all over the western hemisphere and reaching out across the Pacific to Asia and perhaps even to certain isolated points across the Atlantic. The choice before Great Britain is either to become the nucleus of a constellation of power embracing the British Empire and Commonwealth and extending to western Europe, or else to merge herself in one of the other great constellations. Such is the dilemma imposed by the political impact of the Soviet Union and by the economic and financial imperialism of the United States.

Nothing in all this implies the view that power in international affairs has purely material sources. The Soviet leaders in the early days were the first to proclaim the appeal of the revolutionary idea as the source of their strength; and more recently they have freely invoked the idea of the defence of the socialist fatherland as a force capable of sustaining military power. But, in admitting this conception, they would make two reservations. The idea must be associated with, or embodied in, effective power; and the idea itself must not be a mere abstraction, but must take a concrete and material form. In other words, Soviet theory, in proclaiming the power of the idea, postulates a particular kind of ideology. This will be discussed in the next chapter.

V

THE IDEOLOGICAL IMPACT

BOLSHEVISM is no mere political programme, but a philosophy and a creed. Never since the mediaeval church evolved a complete set of rules for human conduct and thought and harnessed to it the temporal power of the emperor, had so bold an attempt been made to establish a comprehensive and coherent body of doctrine covering the whole of man's social, economic, political and intellectual activities and providing the ideological basis for a system of government. The "ideas of 1789" had been, by comparison, limited in scope and fluid in outline—if only because they lacked an authoritative organ to expound and interpret them. Lenin from the very outset emphasized the importance of the party as the custodian of doctrine and of an orthodoxy maintained by rigid discipline; and the system which emerged from the revolution of 1917 established the supremacy of the party, as the repository of orthodoxy, over the state power. This reversed the situation existing in Tsarist Russia—and, logically, in any country possessing an established church—where the state power was supreme, and the body claiming to be the source or exponent of doctrine was subject to the control of the state. Bolshevism has the status of a creed which purports to inspire every act of state power and by which every such act can be tested and

84

judged. Naked and uncontrolled power for the state is no part of Bolshevik doctrine. Bolshevism has shown a remarkable capacity to inspire loyalty and self-sacrifice in its adherents; and this success is beyond doubt due in part to its bold claim —parallel to the claim of the Catholic church in countries where it is paramount—to be the source of principles binding for every form of human activity including the activity of the state.

The mere existence in eastern Europe of a new political order based on a consistent and coherent creed capable of generating this devotion and enthusiasm has had an immense impact on the western world. Even those—or perhaps particularly those—who have rejected most vigorously the content of the creed have been conscious of its power of attraction and of the weakness of a political order lacking the same basis of passionate conviction. This feeling had much to do with the beginnings of fascism and nazism, which proceeded from a conscious reaction against Bolshevism, but also from a scarcely less conscious imitation of it. The moral fervour which Mussolini and Hitler sought to inspire among their followers was a kind of spurious antidote to the fervour of Bolshevism, and many of the methods of Bolshevism were invoked in the attempt to generate it. The impact of this aspect of Bolshevism was felt, however, even in the democratic countries. Democracy everywhere suffered a set-back after the triumph of 1918. This set-back seemed to many the result, not of objective conditions, but of waning enthusiasm; and this was largely due to a feeling that democracy no longer possessed the moral drive, the consistent outlook, the youthful vigour of Bolshevism. In the Britain of the nineteen-thirties, the recall to religion, the demand for a deeper sense of purpose, the appeal of Marxism to young intellectuals and pseudo-intellectuals, the belief, irrational and unsupported by knowledge, in the "Soviet paradise", were all in their different ways significant symptoms of this feeling.

Bolshevism, like Christianity or like any other doctrine which has made a powerful impact on the world, has two aspects: the destructive or revolutionary, and the constructive or positive. Broadly speaking the tendency in any great movement is for the revolutionary aspect to predominate in the earlier stages, the positive aspect in the later. Primitive Christianity was revolutionary until it had disrupted the old Roman civilization; then it created a new and positive world order of its own, and underwent a corresponding modification of its outlook. The Reformation began by being revolutionary and destructive, and ended by becoming the basis of a new social order. Bolshevism has passed, or is passing, through the same two phases; and both have had their impact on the western world. The revolutionary element of Marxist ideology may be considered under three heads—its materialism, its dialectical character, and its relativism.

Materialism, though its metaphysical implications are politically neutral, has been associated in modern times with the tradition of revolution. Materialism, combined with the absolute or static rationalism of the 18th century, was the philosophy of the French revolution. Materialism, combined with the dialectical and relativist rationalism of Hegel, gave birth to Marxism which provided the philosophical background of the Russian revolution. Revolutionary materialism was a revolt both against Christianity and against a metaphysical idealism which believed in spiritual values and pure ideas as the ultimate reality behind the material universe. Translated into political terms, it attacked the privileged classes by alleging that their preoccupation with men's souls masked a convenient and profitable neglect of the needs of men's bodies —when the men concerned belonged to the unprivileged class. Hence Marxism taught that the ultimate reality was material and, above all, economic.

Men make their own history [wrote Engels, summarizing the doctrine in the last year of his life], but in a given environment in which they live, upon the foundation of extant relations. Among these relations, economic relations, however great may be the influence exercised on them by other relations of a political and ideological order, are those whose action is ultimately decisive, forming a red thread which runs through all the other relations and enables us to understand them.

No one can doubt the enormously increased popularity and influence of such conceptions in the modern world. To improve the material standards of living of the masses is today a mission commanding the same kind of moral fervour as formerly went into the task of winning their souls. We have travelled far from primitive Christian conceptions of the wickedness of the material world and of the importance of avoiding and resisting its temptations. The social functions of the church have received a new and revolutionary emphasis. The kind of theology popular in the 19th century which promised rewards hereafter as compensation for the sufferings of this world—what came to be derisively dubbed "pie in the sky"—fell into disrepute. Modern churchmen have been known to argue that the cure of men's souls cannot be successfully undertaken in isolation from the cure of their bodies; and a well-known free church weekly describes itself as a "Journal of Social and Christian Progress". In the academic sphere the immense expansion of economic studies in the last thirty years, and the corresponding decline of philosophy and the humanities, are minor signs of the times. Whether the result be attributed to the impact of Marxism, or of the Soviet Union, or to the rising political consciousness of the unprivileged class, or merely to the increasing stringency of material conditions, greater prominence is given in contemporary life and thought than ever before to the economic foundations of the social order.

The Marxist philosophy was not only materialistic, but dialectical. This character it derived from Hegel's dialectical idealism. According to this doctrine the world moves forward through a continuous interplay and conflict of ideas; one idea, or thesis, is contradicted and assailed by its antithesis, and out of this struggle comes not the victory either of thesis or of antithesis, but a new synthesis; the synthesis is thus established as a thesis, and the process of contradiction begins once more. This state of flux, or historical process, is the ultimate reality: it is also rational, since it is moving forward along certain lines which can be determined by rational investigation. This was what Hegel called the dialectic, and Marx, in substituting the conflict of classes and their material interest for the Hegelian conflict of ideas, preserved the rest of the Hegelian structure intact. Indeed the principles of conflict and flux occupy in the Marxist system a more central place than the materialism. Whether directly from Hegel, or through Marx, or through other channels, the dialectical conception has deeply penetrated western thought since the latter part of the 19th century. Among its symptoms are the belief in perpetual conflict substituted for the belief in a natural harmony of interests; the recognition that social phenomena are not static, but dynamic, and must be studied not as fixed states, but as processes; and the emphasis on history as the key to reality. In the 18th century, philosophy took over from religion the function of explaining the nature of reality. In the 19th century this role was passed on from philosophy to history.

Belief in the historical process, in never-ceasing flux, as the ultimate reality should logically preclude belief in any absolute outside it. The course of history being predetermined by laws of its own is an absolute in its own right, and all that man has to do is to conform to those laws and to help to fulfil them. Hegel, the real inventor of what came to be known to German philosophers as *Historismus*, preached that freedom consisted in the recognition and voluntary acceptance of necessity. This form of historical determinism is the basis of what may be called the "scientific" side of Marx's teaching: the contradictions of capitalism made socialism demonstrably inevitable. "When Marxists organize the communist party and lead it into battle", wrote Bukharin, "this action is also an expression of historical necessity which finds its form precisely through the will and the actions of men." [1] It has sometimes been suggested that to portray history as a chain of events developing one out of the other by an inevitable process is to deprive human beings of all incentive to action. This is good logic but poor psychology. Men like to work for a cause which they think certain to win; conversely, there is no surer way of sapping an adversary's morale than to persuade him that he is bound to lose. Marxism has derived an enormous accretion of strength from the belief that the realization of its predictions is historically inevitable. To have history on one's side is the modern equivalent of being on the side of the angels.

This belief in history is a fundamental tenet of Bolshevism. Both Lenin and Trotsky frequently personified—not to say, deified—history. "History will not forgive us", wrote Lenin on the eve of the Bolshevik revolution, "if we do not seize power now." What is right is to assist the historical process to develop along its predestined lines: what is wrong is to oppose or impede that process. The victory of the proletariat, being scientifically inevitable, is also morally right. The

[1] N. Bukharin, *Historical Materialism* (English trans.), p. 51.

89

French revolutionaries had adopted the slogan *salus populi suprema lex;* Plekhanov, the Russian Marxist, was logical and consistent when he translated this into *salus revolutiae* [sic] *suprema lex.*[1] The revolution was the fulfilment of the historical process: everything that aided history to fulfil itself was right. Ethics could have no other basis and no other meaning. Like other totalitarian philosophies and religions, Bolshevism inevitably tends to justify the means by the end. If the end is absolute, nothing that serves that end can be morally condemned.

The emphasis on history leads on to the third revolutionary element in Marxism, its relativism. The laws of nature are absolute and timeless—or were until recently regarded as such. The laws of the social sciences are embedded in history and conditioned by it: what is true of one period is obviously not true of another. There is no such thing as democracy in the abstract: the nature of democracy depends on the historical development of the society in which it is established, and the application of the same formal rules will yield different results in different social environments. No laws of economics are universally true without regard to time or place. There are classical economics based on the broad pre-suppositions of *laissez-faire,* the economics of "imperfect competition" or monopoly capitalism, and the economics of socialism or the planned society; and different principles will apply to each. Conceptions like "freedom" and "justice" remain abstract and formal until we are able to place them in a concrete historical setting, and bring them to earth by answering the questions "freedom for whom, and from what" or "justice for whom and at whose expense". Not only every social or political institution, but every social and political idea changes with the historical context, or, more specifically, with changes in

[1] G. V. Plekhanov, *Works,* XII (in Russian), pp. 418–19.

90

the relations of productive forces. Reality is never static; everything is relative to a given stage in the historical process.

This thorough-going relativism is ideologically the most destructive weapon in the Marxist armoury. It can be used to dissolve all the absolute ideas on which the existing order seeks to base its moral superiority. Law is not law in the abstract, but a set of concrete rules enacted by an economically dominant class for the maintenance of its privileges and authority. *Bourgeois* law is largely concerned with the protection of the property rights of the *bourgeoisie:* "law and order", though good things in the abstract, become a traditional slogan by which those in possession seek to discredit strikers, revolutionaries and other rebels against the existing social order, however oppressive that order may be. Equality in the abstract is purely formal. "One man, one vote" does not ensure actual equality in a society where one voter may be a millionaire and another a pauper; even equality before the law may be a mockery when the law is framed and administered by the members of a privileged class. Freedom itself can be equally formal. Freedom to choose or refuse a job is unreal if freedom to refuse is merely tantamount to freedom to starve. Freedom of opinion is nullified if social or professional pressures render the holding of some opinions lucrative and expose the holders of other opinions to an economic boycott. Freedom of the press and of public meeting are illusory if the principal organs of the press and the principal meeting-places are, as is inevitable in capitalist society, controlled by the moneyed class. Thus the supposed absolute values of liberal democracy are undermined by the corrosive power of the Marxist critique: what was thought of as absolute turns out to be relative to a given social structure and to possess validity only as an adjunct to that structure. These views have made enormous headway in the last 25 years. To discuss history in constitutional terms, or in terms of a struggle for liberty, democracy or some other abstract ideal, is today almost as old-fashioned as to discuss it in terms of kings and battles. Under the impact of Marxism the study of history has everywhere been placed on sociological foundations. If the 18th century rationalists substituted philosophy for religion, and Hegel substituted history for philosophy, Marx carried the process one stage further by substituting sociology for history.

But the inroads of relativism go deeper still. If the institutional pattern of society and the ideals which animate it are conditioned by the material—or specifically by the economic —foundations on which the society rests, so also are the thought and action of its individual members. Marxism finally deprived the individual of his individuality and made him, first and foremost, the member of a class. What the individual *bourgeois* thought and believed and did was not—or at any rate not merely—the product of his own thinking and volition, but of the conditions imposed on him by his membership of the *bourgeoisie*. Relativism thus becomes the vehicle of a complete scepticism. It is the culmination—or, perhaps, the *reductio ad absurdum*—of the great movement of human thought initiated by Descartes, who made the thinking individual the fixed starting point of his system: *cogito ergo sum.* The achievement of the Enlightenment is thus brought to nought. "Dare to be wise! Dare to use your own intelligence! That is the motto of the Enlightenment." [1] But now human reason, having challenged and destroyed all other values, ends by turning the same weapons against itself. Individualism, having challenged and destroyed the authority of other sources of value and set up the individual judgment as the ultimate source, carries the argument to its logical conclusion and

[1] Kant, *Werke* (ed. Cassirer), IV, p. 169.

proves that this source also is tainted. The process of debunking is pursued to the point where the debunker is himself debunked. The reason of the individual can have no independent validity. His thinking is conditioned by his social situation, and that situation is in turn determined by the stage reached in the historical process.

This weapon can be wielded with devastating force. If pressed home, it would lead to a rejection of all absolute truth or at any rate of all human capacity to know it. Nothing would be true except in relation to a particular situation or a particular purpose, and nothing could be known except from an angle of approach which inevitably makes all knowledge purely subjective. Marxist and Soviet criticism has, however, not been concerned to pursue the matter to this extreme and logical conclusion, but rather to use relativism as a weapon to discredit and dissolve the theories and values of *bourgeois* civilization. The sting of the theory of "conditioned thinking" is that it is so largely true. Obviously few individuals in fact think for themselves; obviously, too, their thinking is in large measure unconsciously conditioned by their social and national background and by their desire to find justification in theory for the practice which the pursuit of their interests demands. It requires no great skill to demonstrate that the political and economic theories which have been fashionable at different periods of history and in different countries reflect the views and the interests of the dominant group at the time and place in question. "Intellectual production", as the *Communist Manifesto* brutally puts it, "changes with material production"; and "the ruling ideas of any particular age have always been merely the ideas of its ruling class". Perhaps the extreme self-confidence and self-satisfaction characteristic of the period of *bourgeois* supremacy, especially in the English-speaking world, made it peculiarly vulnerable to attack. More certainly, the decline in that supremacy, and the challenge presented to it by the first world war and by its consequences, of which the Bolshevik revolution was the most significant, spread the impression that there were hitherto undetected chinks in the armour of *bourgeois* theory. There can be no doubt that the Marxist critique, and the weapon of relativism which it released, was a powerful factor in that wave of general debunking of *bourgeois* values which reached its climax between the two world wars. Few intelligent democrats today deny the validity of some aspects of the Marxist onslaught. The impact of the Soviet Union in the last twenty-five years has helped to drive it home; and Soviet prestige has in turn been increased by the recognition of its validity.

This then is the essence of the revolutionary or destructive impact of Marxism on the western world. A true revolution is never content merely to expose the abuses of the existing order, the cases in which its practice falls short of its precept, but attacks at their root the values on which the moral authority of the existing order is based. Thus Christianity was not so much concerned to denounce the cruelties or injustices of Roman rule as to challenge the principle of authority represented by it. The Reformation did not merely denounce ecclesiastical abuses and misdeeds; it attacked the principle which found the ultimate source of authority in a visible church and its head. The French revolution was not content to arraign individual kings and ministers as wicked; it struck at the principle of royal sovereignty. The gravamen of the Marxist revolution is not that it has exposed the failures and shortcomings of western democracy, but that it has called in question the moral authority of the ideals and principles of western democracy by declaring them to be a reflexion of the interests of a privileged class. The serious thing about the contemporary revolution is not that Marxism has kindled and

94

inflamed the resentments of the under-privileged against the existing order and helped to make them articulate: the serious thing is that it has undermined the self-confidence of the privileged by sapping their own faith in the sincerity and efficacy of the principles on which their moral authority rested.

.   .   .   .   .

All this is the negative or destructive side of the impact of the Marxist and Soviet ideologies on the western world. Such criticism successfully undermines the adversary's position, but does nothing to establish one's own. Indeed consistent relativism, by attacking every absolute, renders any position untenable. It is true that some 19th century thinkers, following the impulsive example of Proudhon, who wrote "I deny all absolutes, I believe in progress", attempted to make progress itself their absolute. Moreover this attempt drew a certain scientific colouring from some of the cruder interpretations of Darwinian evolution. But progress itself is meaningless in the absence of some absolute standard—there is nothing to distinguish progress from regression; and most 19th century believers in progress consciously or unconsciously postulated Tennyson's "far-off divine event, to which the whole creation moves". Marx, for all his belief in the historical process and in the scientific quality of his predictions, made no pretence of being neutral. He had a robust constitution which indulged freely in the luxury of moral judgments. Though the thoughts and actions of individuals were conditioned by their social situation, he was fully prepared to censure or praise them on what were in all seeming moral grounds. Though the victory of the proletariat was scientifically inevitable, Marx implicitly encouraged men to work for it on the ground that it was morally right. The moral undertones, which are never far beneath the surface in Marx, became overtones in the current Soviet ideology. The change is significant for the evolution of Bolshevism from a destructive and revolutionary force into a positive and constructive force. The charge of inconsistency, of a departure from original Marxist orthodoxy, is paralleled in the history of all revolutions which "settle down" and become the basis of a new social order. Every established social order needs its absolutes.

The absolute value which Marxist and Soviet ideology have to offer and to which all else is subordinated is the emancipation of the proletariat, the establishment of its supremacy at the expense of other classes and the ultimate attainment of classless society. The word "proletarian" by its derivation means no more than the unclassed, the under-privileged or the underdog, in whose name all revolutions are made. But it was a stroke of insight which enabled Marx to perceive that the industrial worker, the "wage-slave", was the characteristic "proletarian" of the industrial age, and must be the bearer and the eponymous hero of the next revolution. Just as Hegel abandoned relativism in order to find an absolute in the Prussian nation, so Marx abandoned relativism in order, with better reason, to find his absolute in the proletariat. At the very outset of his career, in 1843, Marx had written that "there is only one class whose wrongs are not specific but are those of the whole society—the proletariat".[1] In the *Communist Manifesto* he implicitly answers the charge that, in becoming the champion of the proletariat, he was merely supporting the cause of one class against another:

All previous movements were movements of minorities or in the interest of minorities. The proletarian movement is the conscious movement of the immense majority in the interest of the immense majority.

[1] Quoted in I. Berlin, *Karl Marx*, p. 87.

The victory of the proletariat, he explained elsewhere in the *Manifesto*, meant not the domination of the proletariat as a class but the end of all class antagonism and the introduction of the classless society. On the tenth anniversary of the Bolshevik revolution Stalin proclaimed the same doctrine:

A revolution in the past generally ended by the replacement at the seat of administration of one group of exploiters by another group of exploiters. The exploiters were changed, the exploitation remained. So it was at the time of the movement for the liberation of the slaves. So it was at the period of the peasant risings. So it was in the period of the well-known "great" revolutions in England, in France, in Germany. . . . The October revolution is different *in principle* from these revolutions. It sets as its goal not the replacement of one form of exploitation by another form of exploitation, of one group of exploiters by another group of exploiters, but the annihilation of every form of exploitation of man by man, the annihilation of every kind of exploiting group, the establishment of the dictatorship of the proletariat, the establishment of the power of the most revolutionary class of all the hitherto existing oppressed classes, and the organization of a new classless socialist society. This is why the *victory* of the October revolution means a radical break in the history of mankind.

The contemporary western ideology of the "common man" doubtless has traditional roots in Christianity and in other revolutionary movements of the past. But it owes its revival and current popularity largely to the impact of Marxism and of the Soviet Union. This is the positive side of the bad conscience generated by the Marxist critique among the *bourgeois* ruling class of the last hundred years. It is the conscience-stricken *bourgeoisie* itself which has shown most eagerness to proclaim "the century of the common man". The "common man" has become an absolute in his own right.

The specific character of the ideal associated with the cult

97

of the proletariat or the common man is social or "socialist" —not using the word in a party sense—in two connotations. It is primarily social as opposed to primarily political in its aims; and it is primarily social as opposed to primarily individual in its values.

In the first place, then, the Bolshevik revolution is primarily social where the French revolution was primarily political. Its concept of social justice is not exhausted by the political ideals of liberty and equality. Of the three ideals of the French revolution, liberty has been tarnished by the discovery that, in default of equality, it remains the privilege of the few; equality by the discovery that, unless it remains purely formal, it can only be achieved through the sacrifice of liberty; and fraternity alone remains, perhaps because little attempt has hitherto been made to give it concrete form. It has been said with more than a grain of truth that the specific ideal of the proletarian revolution is neither liberty nor equality but fraternity. The universality of the Bolshevik appeal, its claim to speak in the name of oppressed groups and classes, both national groups and exploited classes, all over the world, has been a large element in its strength. Even where there has been a retreat in Soviet policy and in Soviet ideology from the unbridled internationalism of the first revolutionary years, the retreat has not been into nationalism of the old-fashioned kind. Soviet nationalism has always claimed to be something different on the ground that it is built up on the brotherhood of the many nations and races composing the Soviet Union.

The strength of Soviet patriotism [said Stalin in one of his war-time speeches] lies in the fact that it is based not on racial or nationalist prejudices but . . . on the fraternal partnership of the working people of all the nations of our country.[1]

[1] Speech of November 6, 1944.

It is not wholly unfair to contrast this new Soviet ideology with the kind of nationalism which, in the western world, has almost always meant the supremacy of a certain national group or groups. It would be difficult to deny that the social and political ideals of the English-speaking world rested until recently, and in some measure still rest, on the unspoken assumption of the superior right of the white man in general, and even of certain sections of the white race in particular. This assumption, which reflects the privileges won by English-speaking countries and a few closely allied nations in the prosperous days of *bourgeois* civilization, is reflected in all the relations of the English-speaking world with the "coloured peoples" and renders those relations peculiarly vulnerable to the Soviet attack. The English-speaking countries have perhaps not been sufficiently sensitive to the threat to their world-wide position implicit in the Soviet appeal to the brotherhood of man; in so far as they have recently become more sensitive to it and have overcome some of the traditional prejudice of race and colour, this is due in large part, directly or indirectly, to the impact of the Soviet Union.

The second and more significant effect of the impact of the Bolshevik ideology has been to hasten the disappearance of the individualist values of *bourgeois* society and the substitution for them of the social values of mass civilization. The age of *bourgeois* capitalism emancipated the individual from his predetermined place in the social and economic order, replaced status by contract, and left the individual free to choose his calling and to rely on his own judgment and his own efforts. The *bourgeois* order brought prosperity and privilege to the capable and enterprising few. Individualism really meant the claim of outstanding individuals to be different, to distinguish themselves by their attainments, and by the enjoyment of corresponding privileges, from the undifferentiated

99

mass of common men. But for the ordinary worker individual freedom to choose his job seemed largely illusory when its complement was freedom to starve. To have no social obligation to work might seem a boon; but it might be purchased at too high a price if society in its turn had no obligation to provide for the workless. The advantages of individualism perhaps never impressed themselves at all deeply on the consciousness of the masses. At any rate by the end of the 19th century the retreat from individualism had begun; the benefits of an assured status once more seemed more alluring than the combination of a partly fictitious independence with a real and intolerable risk. Trade unions, collective bargaining, social insurance and the ever-growing volume of social legislation were symptoms, or perhaps contributory causes, of the retreat from individualism towards the new values of mass civilization. The modern cult of the common man is both broader and bolder in its universality than any previous social programme; for it asserts the social rights not of members of a select society or group but of individual men and women everywhere and without discrimination.

Yet this is not pure gain. The cult of the proletariat, of the common man, by insisting on the equality of social rights common to all, has confirmed the emphasis, already implicit in modern techniques of production, on similarity and standardization. It treats society as a conglomeration of undifferentiated individuals, just as science treats matter as a conglomeration of undifferentiated atoms. The social unit displays a growing determination to "condition" the individuals composing it in uniform ways and for uniform purposes and a growing ability to make this determination effective. The view that the exclusive or primary aim of education is to make the individual think for himself is outmoded; few people any longer contest the thesis that the child should be educated "in" the official ideology of his country. The standardization of production makes it necessary for large numbers of individuals to spend their working hours doing exactly the same thing in exactly the same way. Press and radio ensure that they are inoculated with the same ideas or with a few simple variants of them; commercial advertising strives to make them want the same things to eat, drink and wear, and the same amusements to distract them. The individual becomes depersonalized; the machine and the organization are more and more his masters. The contemporary problem of individualism in a mass civilization has no precedent anywhere in history.

All this has often been described and analysed, and is quite independent of anything that has happened in Russia in the last thirty years. The strong point about the Soviet ideology is that it has been framed in response to the new conditions of mass civilization, and that it has arisen in a country where the sense of community has always been more active than the sense of individual rights. It is therefore far more of a piece than the confused and conflicting beliefs which arise in the west from the attempt to reconcile past and present. The trend towards mass civilization seems irresistible and irreversible; the alternatives are to accept it or to let contemporary civilization perish altogether. But how much of the individualism of the past can be embodied in the collective forms of the present is an unsolved problem. It looks as if the western world will have to develop a stronger sense of the duty of the individual to society, and the Soviet Union a stronger sense of the obligations of society to the individual. Even in the early 1920's Lenin recognized the impracticability of collective management in industry and insisted on a return to one-man management and one-man responsibility. In the 1930's Stalin spoke on several occasions of the dangers of "depersonalization" and of the importance of individual initiative—once, significantly enough, in a much-quoted speech of 1935 at the Red Army Academy at a time when strenuous efforts were being made to increase the prestige and efficiency of the officer corps. In the previous year in his interview with Mr. H. G. Wells he had denied the existence of any "irreconcilable contrast between the individual and the collective, between the particular personality and the interest of the collective". He went on:

> Socialism does not deny individual interests but reconciles them with the interests of the collectivity. . . . The fullest satisfaction can be given to these individual interests only by a socialist society. Moreover a socialist society alone presents a solid guarantee for the protection of the interests of the individual.[1]

These generalizations do not carry us far. But they show the Soviet leaders increasingly aware of the problems of mass civilization in its relation to the individual. In the western world, and particularly in Great Britain, the individualist tradition is so strong and ingrained that the phenomena of mass civilization are often approached not merely without sympathy, but with mistrust and dislike. This does not help; and it has still to be proved that individual enterprise and individual distinction are necessarily crushed out of existence by the far-reaching organization, the external standardization and, perhaps, external drabness which go with mass civilization. Certainly the Soviet Union has gone some way to maintain and develop these qualities even within the framework of a discipline far more rigid than the western world is likely to require or accept. The age-long problem of the place of the individual in society and of the relation of society to the individual is once more on the agenda; and it will have to be worked out in the west, as well as in the Soviet Union, in terms of the mass civilization of the contemporary world.

[1] Stalin, *Leninism* (10th Russian edition), p. 602.

VI

SOME HISTORICAL PERSPECTIVES

THE first millennium of our era saw a constant series of migrations from east to west, from Asia to Europe. Then, as what are called the Dark Ages passed into the Middle Ages, the influx was stayed; and though Russia continued to wrestle with the invading Tartar, and the Turk was driving his fangs into Europe as late as the 17th century, Europe was no longer subject to any large-scale infiltration of men and ideas from the east. Then, as the Middle Ages in turn gave place to the modern period, a Europe re-invigorated by Renaissance and Reformation began to strike outwards; and in three centuries the movement of expansion which had its centre in western Europe had spread over the greater part of the world.

Part of this expansion of Europe took the form of a *Drang nach Osten* from western and central Europe into the still half-civilized regions of eastern Europe. Among its forerunners was the advance of the Teutonic Knights (not all of them Teuton, or at any rate not all German) along the shores of the Baltic; the vast and short-lived Lithuanian Empire reaching to the Black Sea; and the Polish invasions of Russia in the early 17th century. But the effective penetration of Russia by the west began with Peter the Great, who conquered the Baltic provinces and founded Petersburg, thereby, in the famous phrase, "opening a window on Europe"; and through this window European influences poured into Russia, shaping Russian history for good or evil for more than two hundred years. French intellectuals brought to the Russian ruling classes the rationalist and cosmopolitan doctrines of the Enlightenment; Italian architects left their mark in the palaces and mansions of Petersburg and beyond; and British merchants, who had made their first contacts with Russia as early as the 16th century, were succeeded by British engineers and technicians of all kinds. But by far the most powerful influence came from Germany. The dynasty was predominantly German in blood; the court was German; the German ruling class in the Baltic provinces provided an altogether disproportionate share of able generals and administrators; and the whole of Russian official life in the 19th century had acquired a strong Germanic tinge. Finally in the latter part of the 19th century came the economic transformation of Russia by western industrial techniques and western capitalist finance—a process not yet completed in 1914.

These two hundred years of peaceful infiltration of Europe into Russia were punctuated by one dramatic attempt at military conquest, dramatically repulsed. Napoleon's failure at Moscow had far-reaching consequences in Russian history. It gave the signal for the emergence of a Russian national political consciousness, such as had hitherto hardly existed, comparable with the nationalisms of western Europe; and this betokened the beginnings of a reaction against European penetration and a resentment of European influence and European airs of superiority. Russian 19th century history thus bears a dual stamp. It was the period when the impact on Russia for the material civilization of western Europe reached its height, and Russia became in outward semblance more European than at any previous time. It was also the period of a conscious and widespread cult of Russian separateness from Europe, and of the development of a characteristically national and intensely original Russian literature. This duality was expressed in the long controversy between "westerners" and "Slavophils" which ran through so much of Russian 19th century literature and thought. The westerners, representing the tradition of European penetration, believed that all that was vital and progressive in Russian life came from western Europe and that the task of Russian thinkers and Russian statesmen was to make up the time-lag *vis-à-vis* European civilization which Russia's belated cultural and economic development had imposed on her. The Slavophils held that Russia was the home of a native Slav tradition which stood in many respects higher than European civilization and had an irreplaceable contribution to make to it. It was the Slavophils who developed a "messianic" view of Russia's destiny and believed that Moscow, as "the third Rome", would become the source of enlightenment and regeneration for a decadent Europe. Dostoevsky, who did much to popularize Slavophil doctrines, prophesied in a letter of March 1, 1868, that within a hundred years the whole world would be regenerated by Russian thought.

The same ambivalence which ran through Russian 19th century history marked the Bolshevik revolution. In one aspect it was a culmination of the westernizing process, in another a revolt against European penetration. The first Bolsheviks remained impenitent westerners: for them Russia was a backward country to be regenerated by revolutionary doctrines derived from the west. The early Bolsheviks were also whole-hearted internationalists who believed that the "workers had no country" and regarded the Russian revolution merely as part of a European or world-wide revolution. But when, in the middle 1920's, the objective of "socialism in one country" replaced world revolution, the emphasis gradually changed. In the 1930's it became fashionable, both in the Soviet Union and abroad, to assert the continuity of Russian history and the glories of the Russian past; and it was possible with a slightly fanciful ingenuity to detect an analogy between the ideals of Bolshevism and the messianic conceptions of the old Slavophils. Did not both teach that a vigorous and unspoiled Russia, in revolt against the decadent civilization of the west, was destined to lead the world by the force of its ideas along the path of regeneration and progress? From this point of view the popular comparison between Peter the Great and Stalin is hardly apt. Each inaugurated an epoch—Peter that of European penetration of Russia, Stalin that of Russian penetration of Europe.

If this view is correct, the Bolshevik revolution must be regarded, irrespective of the validity of the doctrines which it promulgated, as one of the great turning-points in history. Stalingrad and the defeat of Hitler, reproducing on a vaster scale the impact on Russian national consciousness of the downfall of Napoleon, completed what the Bolshevik revolution had begun. The west-east movement of the past 250 years has been arrested; the world may well stand on the threshold of a renewal of an east-west movement of men and ideas. Politics cannot be understood without reference to material power; and while numbers are not by themselves decisive, power depends among other things on numbers. As Lenin once said, "politics begin where the masses are, not where there are thousands, but where there are millions, that is where serious politics begin"; [1] and a few statistical pointers will help to explain why an arrest of the west-east movement in Europe, and the substitution of an east-west movement, was foreshadowed in the 19th century and came to pass in the 20th. In 1800 the Slavs are believed to have constituted about

[1] Lenin, *Selected Works*, VII (English trans.), p. 295.

a quarter of the population of Europe; on the eve of the second world war they formed nearly a half; by 2000, if present trends continue, two-thirds of the population of Europe will be Slavs. Of the Slav population of Europe about two-thirds are Russians, and this proportion remains fairly constant. Hitler's campaign of 1941 may be regarded as a last desperate fling to maintain the *Drang nach Osten* against odds that were rapidly lengthening. Its ignominious failure opened the way for the new *Drang nach Westen*.

.　　.　　.　　.　　.

The east-west movement may take one of two different forms—direct military and political action, or the peaceful penetration of ideas.

Nothing in the Russian tradition supports a policy of military action in Europe beyond the eastern zone; and the failure of Napoleon and Hitler against Russia provides a warning, which will not easily be forgotten, against military adventures in the converse direction. Western and central Europe possesses no important natural resources required by the Soviet Union, and contains large industrial populations used to fairly high standards of living which the Soviet Union might find it difficult to digest, though these considerations do not apply to certain regions of Asia which may attract Soviet ambitions. In general, the social and economic system of the Soviet Union, offering—as it does—almost unlimited possibilities of internal development, is hardly subject to those specific stimuli which dictated expansionist policies to capitalist Britain in the 19th century, and may dictate such policies to the capitalist United States in the 20th. This is one reason why the economic motive has played a smaller part in the foreign policy of the Soviet Union than in that of any other leading Power.

It cannot seriously be questioned that security is, and will

107

remain for some time to come, the predominant motive of Soviet policy in Europe. The bitterness caused by the attacks launched on Soviet Russia from the west in the first years of the regime has been revived and intensified by the German invasion. For twenty-five years the quest for security has gone on. It has been pursued by different methods. Down to 1933, while Soviet power was weak, general disarmament was advocated; since about 1934 the people of the Soviet Union have been adjured to build up armaments for their own defence. At some periods, isolation from the internecine wars of the capitalist world has been preached; at others, international organization and co-operation with "peace-loving" capitalist nations. Since 1939 the occupation of strategic outposts as bulwarks of security—a method much practised in the past by Great Powers—has entered more and more prominently into Soviet calculations. In eastern Europe this has taken the form of seeking to create a broad protective belt of friendly states which will be impervious to influences hostile to the Soviet Union. The western frontier of this belt coincides roughly with that of the Slav world; but the inclusion in it of Finland and Roumania shows that strategic rather than racial considerations are decisive. What concerns the Soviet Government, first, foremost and all the time, is that this area should be under the control of governments which will provide an effective guarantee against the interference in their affairs of any other Great Power. The experience of the first years of the revolution, when these countries were used as a springboard for launching civil war with the backing of the western Powers against the Soviet regime, is still vividly present in the Russian mind. These regions are for the Soviet Union today what the Monroe Doctrine is for the United States, the Low Countries for Great Britain, or the Rhine frontier for France. But there is nothing in Soviet policy so far to suggest that the east-west movement is likely to take the form of armed aggression or military conquest.

The peaceful penetration of the western world by ideas emanating from the Soviet Union has been, and seems likely to remain, a far more important and conspicuous symptom of the new east-west movement. *Ex Oriente lux*. Recent emphasis on the continuity of Russian history, which tends to depict the revolution of 1917 as a sort of incidental exuberance on a broad majestic stream, may lead to one of two erroneous conclusions. The first is to treat Bolshevism as a specifically Russian phenomenon without significance for western civilization. The second is to treat the influence of Bolshevism on the western world as the impact of an alien and unfamiliar eastern ideology. Both these views are misleading. Many specific events and developments in the Soviet Union bear no doubt the peculiar stamp of the Russian past. It is possible to find the prototype of the collective farm in the old Russian peasant community, the *mir*, or to trace back the Cheka and the G.P.U. to the bodyguard of Ivan the Terrible. It can be convincingly argued that Russia had never developed the strong strain of individualism which had entered into western tradition with the Renaissance and the Reformation, and was therefore likely to be more receptive to the ideas and practices of a mass civilization. But Bolshevism itself has western origins and a framework of reference in western thought and life. It lies, not less than the French revolution, in the main stream of European history and has beyond doubt its relevance and its lessons for the western world.

The contemporary crisis of western civilization is in, perhaps, its profoundest aspect, the crisis of the individual. The age of individualism now drawing to its close stands in history as an oasis between two totalitarianisms—the totalitarianism of the mediaeval church and empire and the new totalitarianism of the modern world. If individualism be defined as the belief that the individual mind or conscience is the final human repository of truth, and that every individual must therefore in the last resort make his own judgments, totalitarianism is the belief that some organized group or institution, whether church or government or party, has a special access to truth and therefore the special right and duty of inculcating it on members of the society by whatever means are likely to prove most effective. For four centuries, from 1500 to 1900, individualism was the main driving force of civilization. The Renaissance had revolted against cultural totalitarianism in the name of individual human reason, the Reformation against ecclesiastical totalitarianism in the name of the individual human conscience. The combination of these two potentially discordant elements, the classical and the Christian, stimulated and reinforced by the outstanding success of science in exploring and controlling man's physical environment, and reaching its culmination in the co-called Enlightenment of the 18th century, moulded modern man. Throughout this period the cult of the individual and the belief in his power were so dominant a factor in the religion, the morality, the politics and the economics of the western world that it is still difficult to realize its exceptional character. Yet only once before in human history—in the civilization which was born in 5th century Athens and spread a waning afterglow over the Roman world—had individual man approached this dizzy faith in himself as the centre of the universe. The recovery of this faith through the rediscovery of classical antiquity was the essence of the Renaissance, and heralded the beginning of another great age of human achievement.

What a piece of work is a man! how noble in reason! how infinite in faculty! in form how like an angel! in apprehension how like a god!

For nearly 2,000 years this note had scarcely been heard; from the 16th to the 19th century it was hardly ever silent.

At any time before 1900 it would have been superfluous to recall the immense achievements of this great and productive age—the flowering of artistic and literary creation and the advance of scientific knowledge under the impulse of the new freedom of thought and criticism, the expansion of trade and industry and material well-being, and above all the encouragement given by society to restless individual enterprise and the sense of individual responsibility. But during the first half of the 20th century the tide has turned sharply. The contemporary trend away from individualism and towards totalitarianism is everywhere unmistakable. Social pressures are strongly set towards orthodoxy; conformity is more highly prized than eccentricity. The virtues of what used to be called "sturdy individualism" are overshadowed by threats of "social disintegration". Among the Christian churches those that stem from the individualism of the Reformation are in decline; the only Christian church which still holds its ground is the least individualist and most totalitarian of them all. Of modern political philosophies, Marxism is the most consistently totalitarian and has the widest appeal; the country which has officially adopted it—and which never shared in the individualist tradition of the rest of Europe—has dazzled the world by its immense industrial progress, the spirit of its people and the rapid development of its power. Two world wars, a series of major revolutions, and an economic collapse whose severity was mitigated and curtailed only by wholesale departures from the old individualist tradition, have sufficed to produce a startlingly rapid change of moral climate and to convince all but the blind and the incurable that the forces of individualism have somehow lost their potency and their relevance in the contemporary world.

Seen therefore in the broadest historical perspective, the impact of the Soviet Union on the western world symbolizes the end of that period of history which began in the 16th and 17th centuries and was marked by the world-wide ascendancy of western Europe and, in particular, of the English-speaking peoples. Like other great historical movements, the Bolshevik revolution was self-assertive and highly dramatic in its setting and consequences. But like other great historical movements, it owed its success not merely to its own power and to the enthusiasm which it generated among its disciples, but to the inner crumbling of the order against which it was directed. The impact of the Soviet Union has fallen on a western world where much of the framework of individualism was already in decay, where faith in the self-sufficiency of individual reason had been sapped by the critique of relativism, where the democratic community was in urgent need of reinforcement against the forces of disintegration latent in individualism, and where the technical conditions of production on the one hand, and the social pressures of mass civilization on the other, were already imposing far-reaching measures of collective organization. The ideas which the Soviet impact brought with it thus fell on well-prepared ground; the men of every nation who helped to spread communist ideas in the west were not as a rule venal "fifth columnists" (though these no doubt existed), but men who sincerely saw in those ideas a cure for the evils of their own country. Hence, too, the success of Soviet propaganda, and the important part which it played in the conduct of Soviet foreign policy and in the growth of Soviet power.

How can the western world best meet this challenge presented by the Soviet impact? Clearly the element of power is present; and in so far as the issue is one of power, it will depend on the rival strength, military and economic, of the competitors. But this is a shallow, or at any rate an imperfect, view of the matter. Much will depend on the attitude of those peoples, on the European continent and outside it, who have not made a declared choice between western democracy and communism, and may prefer forms of government intermediate between them; and this attitude will be mainly determined, not by ideological sympathies, but by the economic achievements and social programmes of western democracy and communism respectively. Much will also depend on the extent of the support which the Soviet Union indirectly derives from those men and women in the western world who, diagnosing the evils of western society, believe that some of the ideas inherent in the Bolshevik revolution are relevant to those evils and can be invoked to cure them. The preceding pages have been an attempt to enquire how far this belief is valid. That it has some validity hardly anyone will any longer care to deny; and if this is true, the prospect is probably not an out-and-out victory either for the western or for the Soviet ideology, but rather an attempt to find a compromise, a half-way house, a synthesis between conflicting ways of life. The danger for the English-speaking world lies perhaps most of all in its relative lack of flexibility and in its tendency to rest on the laurels of past achievements. No human institution or order of society ever stands still. The fate of the western world will turn on its ability to meet the Soviet challenge by a successful search for new forms of social and economic action in which what is valid in individualist and democratic tradition can be applied to the problems of mass civilization.

Printed in the United States
136814LV00004B/70/A